"When I was in seminary I discovered these radio addresses by J. Gresham Machen in which... sible and popular presentati... ned doctrine at that. I was f... en. These lucid radio talks ... sts by several years. I have r... es. Their arguments and ill... ...need my preaching. I can't recomm... ...them enough."

—TIMOTHY KELLER, Founding Pastor, Redeemer Presbyterian Church, New York City, NY

"J. Gresham Machen was one of the most prescient and courageous Christian theologians of the early 20th century. During his life, Machen was a clear and consistent voice for Christian orthodoxy and evangelical truth in the face of liberalism. This collection of lectures is a valuable addition to the Machen library. These lectures reflect the heart of Machen's ministry and provide yet another compelling presentation of Apostolic Christianity. Machen's works are as relevant now as they were when they were first written. These lectures are no exception."

—ALBERT MOHLER, President, The Southern Baptist Theological Seminary

"Here is theology that floats like a butterfly and stings like a bee. In these addresses Machen defends a high and biblical view of Christ with punch and quite stunning verve. Fresh, enlightening, and logically compelling, this is not only good theology but a model of good apologetics."

—MICHAEL REEVES, President, Union School of Theology

"These pages constitute treasure that has been hidden far too long—J. Gresham Machen bringing his incisive scholarly mind to bear on the big issues surrounding the person of Christ. As well as clearly expounding Jesus's identity, these pages excel in dismantling false assumptions, muddle-headed and illogical reasoning, and subtle mishandlings of the Scriptures. *The Person of Jesus* is simultaneously a superb primer on the teaching of the Gospels and a powerful illustration of how to 'destroy arguments and every lofty opinion raised against the knowledge of God, and take every thought captive to obey Christ' (2 Cor 10:5)."

—SINCLAIR FERGUSON, Former Senior Minister,
First Presbyterian Church, Columbia, SC

"The life and teaching of J. Gresham Machen are rightly revered by contemporary Christians who prize Reformed orthodoxy. Dr. Machen's compelling voice lives again in the pages of this short book of radio talks on the divine Son of God. As a theologian for ordinary Christians, his clear and concise communication of biblical truth will draw new readers into a deeper and more personal knowledge of the risen Christ."

—PHILIP RYKEN, President, Wheaton College

"During my college years the chapters reprinted in this volume along with other non-academic writings of Machen were a significant influence in my life, and I have returned to them from time to time, always with great profit. Written for his own day, they have lost none of their relevance and will continue to serve the cause of the gospel and the church's wellbeing not only today but for generations to come."

—RICHARD GAFFIN, Emeritus Professor of Biblical and
Systematic Theology, Westminster Theological Seminary

"Dr. Machen's radio addresses on Christ, uttered over eighty years ago, are astonishingly contemporary when read today. . . . To get maximum benefit from this book, read one address per day—praying your way through it for worldwide reformation and revival today."

—**JOEL BEEKE,** President, Puritan Reformed Theological
   Seminary

"With disarming brevity, Machen bracingly pleads with his reader for true belief in the true King of heaven and earth. I understand why even his theological sparring partner, Pearl Buck, respected her orthodox opponent so profoundly. Machen is clearly a spiritual gentleman, a worthy scholar, and a tender shepherd. . . . Machen may well have no peer when it comes to clear, direct, and stirring expositional and applicational writing. Reader, prepare your mind and heart for a bracing read."

—**JOSEPH NOVENSON,** Senior Teaching Pastor, Lookout
   Mountain Presbyterian Church, Lookout Mountain, TN

"J. Gresham Machen is one of a select band of Christian writers of whom it can truly be said that 'he being dead, yet speaketh.' This reprint of some of his most important talks will be widely welcomed by those who appreciate his strong and learned defense of orthodoxy, and it will make his thought more accessible to a younger generation."

—**GERALD BRAY,** Research Professor of Divinity,
   Beeson Divinity School

"This work certainly is a classic jewel. A 'classic' because, even though it dates back to 1935, this book is still fresh and relevant. A 'jewel' because it presents the person and work of Jesus Christ so clearly, convincingly, and appealingly to the reader. Dr. Machen's voice can be heard again and we do well to listen to it."

—**HERMAN SELDERHUIS,** Director, Refo500

"This powerful little book on the deity of Christ fully displays what made Machen great. We see his relentless logic in the clarity of his thinking and the lucidity of his prose. The Gospels leave us no doubt that Jesus Christ is fully God, and Machen demonstrates that any other interpretation falls to the ground."

—THOMAS SCHREINER, James Buchanan Harrison Professor
of New Testament Interpretation, The Southern Baptist
Theological Seminary

"Dr. Machen's talks are timeless, though set in the swirling currents of his day, because the Christ he described, the Christ revealed in the Scriptures by the Spirit, rises above time. His learned rhetoric, his passionate defense of Christian orthodoxy, his love of the Savior and his church make what you will find in these pages a delight to read, a source of spiritual strengthening, and a bulwark against the destructive effects of a contemporary scholarship that continues to denigrate the Creator, Redeemer, and only Judge of mankind."

—JOHN HANNAH, Distinguished Professor of Historical
Theology, Dallas Theological Seminary

"These addresses on the person of Christ were forged long ago in the furnace of debate. They are, however, as fresh today, and as compelling, as they were when they were first delivered. Machen speaks with clarity, conviction, a matchless command of the subject, and with the wind of historic Christianity behind him."

—DAVID WELLS, Distinguished Research Professor,
Gordon-Conwell Theological Seminary

"Throughout his life, J. Gresham Machen wrestled with questions over the relationship between history and faith, between Jesus and Paul. Here in these radio addresses, we have his warm and winsome answers to those questions. . . . It is a great gift to the church that these radio addresses are now being published; take up and read—be refreshed and strengthened in our common faith."

—SEAN MICHAEL LUCAS, Professor of Church History,
Reformed Theological Seminary, Jackson

"Many know of Machen's scholarly achievement and powerful support for historic Christianity over modern substitutes. Less well-known is his ability to convey what is lofty and profound in the simplest of terms. This little book restates the Bible's depiction of God the Son in language easy to grasp. . . . Machen's remarks are as timely now as when first uttered. This is a superb survey of New Testament Christology and a powerful invitation to (re)discover the true Jesus, still Lord despite generations of naysayers and the complacency of his church."

—ROBERT YARBROUGH, Professor of New Testament,
Covenant Theological Seminary

"Sanity regained in a world gone mad. J. Gresham Machen flows with a heart of love for the Lord Jesus. Cool, clear, and fresh as a mountain stream, he bubbles with living water. Doctrinal indifference, a big issue in his day, is the black plague of ours. The antidote to truth decay is his clarity about who Jesus was, what he said and did, and, above all, how he lives and reigns today."

—PAUL WELLS, Emeritus Professeur, Faculté Jean Calvin

"These gems by J. Gresham Machen are essential reading now for thoughtful Christians. Historians of conservative Protestantism will also greatly benefit from these addresses. . . . In these talks, Machen distills the core doctrines about the person and work of Christ that he fought so hard to defend against the acids of modernity. Listen for Machen's voice as you read these transcriptions. Lend your ear to this man whose apologetic labors hastened his tragic, early death."

—**Douglas Sweeney,** Professor of Church History and the History of Christian Thought, Trinity Evangelical Divinity School

"J. G. Machen was the towering intellectual defender of historic Christianity during one of the most turbulent periods in American church history. . . . These talks on the person of Jesus, delivered in the heat of the battle, are not merely an important theological voice from the past; they will encourage your faith today."

—**Frank James,** President, Biblical Theological Seminary

"Almost eighty years after his death, J. Gresham Machen's voice still speaks with clarity and timeliness concerning the person of Christ. In our time, when people question whether Christians and Muslims worship the same God, Dr. Machen's cogent exposition of Scripture in these radio addresses from 1935 provides needed clarity concerning the triune God and the deity of Christ."

—**William Barker,** Emeritus Professor of Church History, Westminster Theological Seminary

"J. Gresham Machen was one of the best thinkers and writers among Reformed theologians before his untimely death on New Year's Day of 1937. . . . Machen's writing is always crisp and clear, without any compromise of cogent argument. . . . When Machen finishes dealing with an unbelieving argument, I always feel that there is nothing more to be said on the unbelieving side.

Even though this work is over eighty years old now, I would not hesitate to give it to someone who had doubts as to the deity of Christ, his miracles, and his resurrection."

—**JOHN FRAME**, Professor of Systematic Theology and Philosophy, Reformed Theological Seminary, Orlando

"All of the qualities that enabled J. Gresham Machen to make such an important contribution to English-speaking Protestantism—theological tenacity, clarity of mind, readability, and courageous conviction—are easy to see in this instructive and edifying collection of radio addresses on the person of Christ. These talks show once again that doctrine has consequences, with Machen as a superbly gifted guide to the significance of what the church confesses about Christ."

—**D. G. HART**, Author of *Defending the Faith: J. Gresham Machen and the Crisis of Conservative Protestantism in Modern America*

"Dr. J. Gresham Machen was one of the lions of reformed evangelical thought in the twentieth century. His clarity of thought and courage borne of a deep conviction and a personal walk with the God about whom he spoke and wrote suffuses every one of these fine radio addresses. . . . With disarming simplicity they present the most important truths in the world and challenge us all to take them seriously. We need more of such clarity and directness today."

—**MARK THOMPSON**, Principal, Moore Theological College

"Tight in argument yet pastoral in exhortation! What a treat! The revival of the uniqueness of Christ is to rediscover the gospel for today. The publication of Dr. Machen's *The Person of Jesus* is an excellent contribution by Westminster Seminary Press, considering that the theological climate in Asia, let alone the whole world, is rapidly growing weak in its grips of who Jesus really is."

—**Kevin Woongsan Kang,** Professor of Systematic Theology, Chongshin University and Theological Seminary

"These popular addresses show the heart of J. Gresham Machen: brilliant, clear, persuasive, calling everyone to faith and life in Jesus. They will bless and encourage all who read them."

—**W. Robert Godfrey,** President, Westminster Seminary California

"J. Gresham Machen was a man of his times, enmeshed in protracted and penetrating conflict over the triumphant liberalism of his day. He was also a man who transcended his times, because he undertook, with rare learning and clear-sighted understanding, the defense of the faith 'once for all entrusted to God's holy people' (Jude 3). His *Christianity and Liberalism*, for instance, written almost a century ago, still sounds amazingly prophetic. This present short volume brings together six of Machen's radio talks of 1935, preserving Machen's voice and emphases in an idiom that is more popular than his large books, but no less important. Machen is always worth reading."

—**D. A. Carson,** Research Professor of New Testament, Trinity Evangelical Divinity School

"This is vintage Machen. He is lucid, logical, and unrelenting in defending what Scripture claims regarding God and the deity of Christ versus modern critics who would explain away or diminish those claims."

—**George Marsden,** Francis A. McAnaney Professor of History Emeritus, University of Notre Dame

"While these addresses, delivered by J. Gresham Machen in 1935, were important in their own time, they are perhaps even more urgent and necessary today. What more important topic is there than the person and work of Christ? Machen, a first-rate scholar, knew how to take the case to the people—and here he does exactly that."

—**STEPHEN J. NICHOLS**, Chief Academic Officer,
Ligonier Ministries

"In these seven brief lectures, Machen follows the main spine of Christian truth. . . . *The Person of Jesus* is Machen's reminder to the church of who we are—a reminder we needed then, and that we need still. In these lectures, the mists of mysticism melt away, and the simple, elegant, profound truths of the Bible appear."

—**MARK DEVER**, Senior Pastor, Capital Hill Baptist Church,
Washington, D.C.

"In J. Gresham Machen, God gave the church an inimitable champion of biblical orthodoxy and gospel clarity. This book will show you why Machen is one of American evangelicalism's most important 20th-century thinkers. More to the point, this book will ground you firmly in what it means to see in the face of Jesus Christ the grace and truth and glory of God."

—**RUSSELL MOORE**, President, Ethics & Religious Liberty
Commission of the Southern Baptist Convention

"This is a superb volume: clear, lucid, precise, and easy to follow. In each chapter, one must not miss that Machen clearly makes his case for the *historical* factuality of Christ's identity on the basis of the *authority* of Scripture. Machen brought the listener—and now the reader—into the serious antithesis between the biblical teaching about Christ and modernism's teaching about Christ.

His sharp, contrasting arguments will always be relevant in the life of the church. Hence, it would be well for Christ's body not to marginalize Machen as a nostalgic symbol. His battle for Christian truth uncovers the folly of those growing increasingly flexible toward broadening the doors of biblical orthodoxy."

—**WILLIAM D. DENNISON**, Professor of Interdisciplinary Studies, Covenant College

"Someone said recently that we need 'a new Machen' to speak insightfully to present-day theological confusions. That would be great. But, thank the Lord, the old Machen does continue to teach us. These wonderful addresses speak powerfully—and with refreshing clarity—to all of us today about the living Christ."

—**RICHARD J. MOUW**, President Emeritus, Fuller Theological Seminary

"I first encountered J. Gresham Machen's work as an undergraduate student grappling with modern challenges to the Christian faith. I found in him a mind passionate for the truth and a heart aflame with the gospel. Both of these traits shine through in these radio talks from the 1930s. We still need to hear what he had to say."

—**TIMOTHY GEORGE**, Dean, Beeson Divinity School

the
PERSON
of JESUS

the

PERSON
of JESUS

✛

*Radio Addresses on the
Deity of the Savior*

J. GRESHAM MACHEN

With a foreword by DAVID POWLISON
And an introduction by JEFFREY JUE

WSP WESTMINSTER
SEMINARY PRESS
Philadelphia, Pennsylvania

To the graduates of Westminster on the mission field,
proclaiming the power of Jesus.

"We cannot afford to lose either the God in the man or the man in the God; our hearts cry out for the complete God-man whom the Scriptures offer us."

—B. B. WARFIELD,
"The Human Development of Jesus"

CONTENTS

FOREWORD

In these talks, J. Gresham Machen uses disarmingly simple words to portray our God. He is speaking with fellow human beings whose welfare matters to him. I will flag three characteristics of how he speaks that can have an impact on how you approach the Christian life and how you go about the ministry of the Word.

First, Machen makes effective use of "lesser to greater" arguments. He points out a common human experience then likens our incomprehensible God to this thing that we easily comprehend. Why is this so significant? It mirrors Jesus's ministry method. Jesus never talks over people's heads. He connects who he is to life. So, for example, a lost coin, a lost sheep, and a lost son help us to get how God himself searches out straying children (Luke 16). The *way* God lifts the veil on himself enables sinful and finite creatures to know him. Machen has modeled his ministry on God's own methods of bringing merciful truth down to earth.

Second, Machen simply listens closely to what Scripture is saying, and then tells us what Scripture says. So how can we know that Jesus is Lord, the Son of God, and divine Messiah? Notice who the prophets were waiting for. Notice how Jesus describes himself. Notice how he prays. Notice how those who lived with him spoke of him. There are probably no ideas here that you haven't heard, read, thought, or said before. But Machen's lucid exposition makes Jesus come forth as fresh as blue sky after days of dismal gray.

Third, this book aims to teach us *doctrine*. It aims that we become *soundly indoctrinated*. Amen and amen! It's curious that Christian faith is criticized for asserting "doctrines," as if that word denotes something arbitrary, narrow-minded, and unquestioning. But every human being and every worldview asserts doctrines. A point of view that someone believes is true—whether about God, or sex, or identity, or other people, or what makes life worthwhile—is a doctrine. And how sad that "indoctrination" has come to only mean something coercive, manipulative, and closed to examining other points of view. No doubt, indoctrinating voices—advertisers, academics, advocates for a cause, family, friends, and religionists—can be coercive, deceptive, and closed. But to be *soundly indoctrinated* is to learn Scripture's gaze and purposes by heart—the very best way to examine all the other points of view, the very best way to tackle any hard questions.

Sit down with these short chapters. Listen to the warm voice of Machen the pastor as he both nourishes and defends your faith. Your loving trust will deepen as you more clearly perceive the Jesus who has loved you.

—David Powlison, PhD
Executive Director
Christian Counseling and Educational Foundation

INTRODUCTION

The radio addresses of Dr. J. Gresham Machen, delivered from January to April in 1935, are a unique and condensed summary of some of the most significant doctrinal issues that Dr. Machen taught and defended throughout his career. By 1935 all of Dr. Machen's major works were published, including: *The Origins of Paul's Religion* (1921), *Christianity and Liberalism* (1923), and *What is Faith?* (1925). These were all written at the height of the controversy between the modernists and fundamentalists in the Presbyterian church, where Dr. Machen set forth with great clarity and scholarly precision the critical issues that divided orthodox Christianity from liberalism. In these works he distinguished himself as a world-class scholar with an uncanny ability to penetrate to the heart of a theological issue and lay bare the consequences.

However, by 1935 his battle against liberalism was slowly being lost. The Presbyterian Church USA's decision to reorganize the Board of Princeton Theological Seminary resulted in the addition of signers of the infamous Auburn Affirmation (a document supporting liberalism). This signaled the demise, for Dr. Machen and others, of this historic seminary. Along with three other professors, Dr. Machen resigned from Princeton and founded Westminster Theological Seminary in 1929. His hope and desire was to continue the legacy of Old Princeton and the defense of confessional orthodox Christianity.

In addition to founding a new seminary, Dr. Machen continued to fight the steady onslaught of liberalism in his denomination. Dr. Machen opposed liberal leaders of the Board of Foreign Missions who were revising the theological purpose for mission work by the PCUSA. According to the liberals, evangelism was no longer the goal of foreign mission, but simply social service. In order to preserve an orthodox Christian mission board that would support and send gospel-preaching missionaries, Machen founded the Independent Board for Presbyterian Foreign Missions in 1933.

The following radio addresses were given in 1935 in the midst of his battles within the church courts over the establishment of the Independent Board for Presbyterian Foreign Missions. Dr. Machen ultimately was suspended from the ministry in 1936, which later compelled him to found a new denomination, the Orthodox Presbyterian Church. Of course he would not have known it at the time, but these radio addresses would be some of his last public words, as he would fall ill and die unexpectedly on January 1, 1937.

In many ways, these addresses are a remarkably concise

summary of the central theological doctrines that J. Gresham Machen defended throughout his valiant fight against liberalism. In these addresses, Dr. Machen answers the questions: who is Jesus Christ, and what did he do? The answers to these questions were the most pressing for Christians in his day, and they are for us as well. Dr. Machen affirmed that Jesus Christ is God incarnate, truly the eternal God united to a human nature, with all divine authority and supernatural power. And Dr. Machen goes to great lengths to demonstrate this truth from numerous texts of Scripture.

For Dr. Machen, Jesus is not a mere man who serves as an ethical example or a teacher of good principles. He is our Savior, and as Dr. Machen stated, "a purely human, or mere natural, as distinguished from a supernatural, Christ can never be our Savior." Jesus Christ, God incarnate, came as the Savior and accomplished salvation, according to Dr. Machen. The final demonstration of Jesus Christ's work was his resurrection. Dr. Machen defends the supernatural bodily resurrection of Jesus Christ, and he asserts that this pivotal historical event evinces the truth of Christianity.

These transcribed radio addresses are commended as a clear and wonderful presentation of the basic orthodox Christian commitments that Dr. Machen embraced and defended. They are delivered by a renowned scholar, but presented in a way that encourages everyone to read and carefully reflect on them. Even more important, they reveal the heart of one called to proclaim the whole counsel of God to a world that desperately needs to hear the truth. Dr. Machen ended his last address with this plea:

> Oh, that God would open men's eyes that they might see, that they might detect the grand sweep and power of his testimony to himself in his Word! Oh, that he would take away the terrible blindness of men's minds! Has he taken away the blindness of *your* minds, my friends? Do you know the risen Christ today as your Savior and your Lord? If you do not yet know him, will you not bow before him at this hour and say, "My Lord and my God!"

No doubt this is as relevant to readers today as it was for Machen's first listeners in 1935.

—Jeffrey K. Jue, PhD
Provost & Executive Vice President
Westminster Theological Seminary

ONE

The Triune God

I wish to open this little series of talks by discussing what the Bible teaches about God. The Bible tells us there is a personal God, Creator and Ruler of the world. God, according to the Bible, is not another name for the mighty process of nature, and he is not some one part or aspect of the process. He is a free and holy person, who created the process of nature by the fiat of his will and who is eternally independent of the universe that he has made.

Now we ask more in detail what the Bible tells us about God. When we ask that, I know we shall be met with an objection. We are seeking to know God. Well, there are many people who tell us that we ought not seek to know God. The knowledge of God, they say, is the death of religion. Instead of seeking to know God, they tell us we ought simply to feel him; putting all theology aside, they say we ought just to sink ourselves in the boundless ocean of God's being.

Such is the attitude of the mystics, ancient and modern. But it is not the attitude of the Christian. The Christian, unlike the mystic, knows him whom he has believed.

What shall be said of a religion that depreciates theology, that depreciates the knowledge of God?

One thing that can be said of it is that it hardly possesses any moral quality at all. Pure feeling, if such a thing exists, is non-moral. That can be observed in the sphere of human relationships. What makes my affection for a human friend such an ennobling thing is the knowledge that I have of the character and the needs of my friend. Am I indifferent to such knowledge? Am I indifferent to base slanders which are directed against my friend's reputation? Not if I am a friend worthy of the name. Human affection, apparently so simple, is in reality just bristling with doctrine; it depends upon a host of observations, stored up in the mind, regarding the object of affection.

That is true, I think, even with regard to those human affections that are often thought of as instinctive. Take, for example, the love of a mother for a child. That love is no doubt independent of excellence in the child; it is impossible to kill a mother's love, no matter what one may do. But is a mother's love independent of some knowledge of the child, independent of some knowledge of the child's sufferings and needs, independent of some ability to enter into the soul of the child in order to sympathize and understand? If it is thus independent of all knowledge, I am inclined to think that it is hardly human affection at all; it has descended to an almost sub-human level.

It is to that sub-human, non-personal level that the mystic seeks to degrade our communion with God. Very different is the love of God as the Bible sets it forth. According to the Bible, we love God because he first loved us; and he has told us of his love in his holy Word. We love God, if we obey what the Bible tells us, because God has made himself known to us and has thus shown himself to be worthy of our love.

I do not mean to say that the Christian in his communion with God is always rehearsing consciously the things that God has told us about himself. There are times, as someone has observed, when a child of God, weary with the battle of life, can say only as he lies down to rest: "Lord, thou knowest, we are on the same old terms." There are times when the Christian can be strangely conscious of the presence of God, even though he is not for the moment thinking in detail about the things that he knows regarding God. Certainly the Bible does offer to us an immediate communion with God, which is like no other experience which a man can possibly have; and certainly the Bible does make a distinction between knowing God and merely knowing about God. But underlying that sweet and blessed communion of the Christian with his God there is a true knowledge of God. A communion with God which is independent of that knowledge of God is communion with some other god and not with the living and true God whom the Bible reveals.

Every true man is resentful of slanders against a human friend. Should we not be grieved ten times more by slanders against our God? How can we possibly listen with polite complacency, then, when men break down the distinction between God and man, and drag God down to man's level? How can we possibly say, as in one way or another is so often said, that orthodoxy makes little difference. We should never talk in any such way about a human friend. We should never say with regard to a human friend that it makes no difference whether our view of him is right or wrong. How, then, can we say that absurd thing with regard to God?

The really consistent Christian can have nothing whatever to do with such doctrinal indifferentism. There is nothing so dishonoring to God, he will say, as to be indifferent to the things that God has told us about himself in his holy Word.

What, then, has God told us about himself in his Word? I certainly cannot now answer that question with any fullness. But there are a few things that I do want to say, and if by saying them I can be helpful to you in your own reading of the Bible, the purpose of this little series of talks will have been attained.

In the Shorter Catechism of the Presbyterian churches, there is the following answer to the question, "What is God?":

God is a Spirit, infinite, eternal, and unchangeable, in His being, wisdom, power, holiness, justice, goodness, and truth. (WSC Q&A 4)

That answer is certainly in accordance with the Bible. I think it will help us a little bit to get straight in our minds what the Bible says about God.

Notice that God is here said to be infinite, eternal, and unchangeable. What is meant by saying that he is infinite? Well, the word "infinite" means without an end or a limit. Other beings are limited; God is unlimited. I suppose it is easy for us to fall into our ordinary spatial conceptions in trying to think of God. We may imagine ourselves passing from the earth to the remotest star known to modern astronomy—many, many light-years away. Well, when we have got there, we are not one slightest fraction of an inch nearer to fathoming infinity than we were when we started. We might imagine ourselves traveling ten million times ten million times farther still, and still we would not be any nearer to infinity than when we started. We cannot conceive a limit to space, but neither can we conceive of infinite space. Our mind faints in the presence of infinity.

But we were really wrong in using those spatial conceptions in thinking of infinity, and particularly wrong were we in using spatial conceptions in thinking of the infinite God. It may help us to the threshold of the truth to say that God pervades the whole vast area of the universe known to science, and then infinitely more; it may help us to the threshold of the truth to say that God inhabits infinite space: but when we look a little deeper we see that space itself belongs to finite things and that the notion of infinite space is without meaning. God created space when he created finite things. He himself is beyond space. There is no near and no far to him. Everything to him is equally near.

So it is when we try to think of God as eternal. If the word "infinity" is related, by way of contrast, to the notion of space, so the word "eternity" is related, by way of contrast, to the notion of time. When we say that God is eternal, we mean that he had no beginning and that he will have no end. But we really mean more than that. We mean that time has no meaning for him, save as it has meaning to the creatures whom he has made. He created time when he created finite creatures. He himself is beyond time. There is no past and no future to him. The Bible puts that in poetical language when it says: "For a thousand years in your sight are but as yesterday when it is past, or as a watch in the night" (Ps 90:4). We of course are obliged to think of the actions of God as taking place in time. We are obliged to think of him as doing one thing after another thing; we are obliged to think of him as doing this today and that tomorrow. We have a perfect right so to think, and the Bible amply confirms us in that right. To us there is indeed such a thing as past and present and future, and when God deals with us he acts in a truly temporal series. But to God himself all things are equally present. There is no such thing as "before" or "after" to him.

It is very important to see clearly that God is thus infinite, eternal, and unchangeable. These attributes of God are often denied. Those who have denied them have told us that God is a finite God. We must not blame him, they tell us, if things are not just right in the world. He is doing the best he can, they say; he is trying to bring order out of chaos, but he is faced by a recalcitrant material which he did not create and which he can mold only gradually and imperfectly to his will. It is our business to help him, and while we may at first sight regret that we have not the all-powerful God that we used to think we had, yet we can comfort ourselves with the inspiring thought that the God that we do have needs our help and indeed cannot do without it.

What shall we say of such a finite God? I will tell you plainly what I think we ought to say about him. He is not God but *a* god. He is a product of men's thoughts. Men have made many such little gods. Of the making of gods, as of the making of books, there is no end. But, as for us Christians, with our Bibles before us, we turn from all such little gods of man's making, out toward the dread mystery of the infinite and eternal, and say, as

Augustine said with a holy fear: "Thou has made us for thyself, and our heart is restless until it finds its rest in thee."

The definition in the Shorter Catechism, which we are taking to give us our outline of what the Bible tells us about God, says not only that God is infinite, eternal, and unchangeable in his being and in his power and in his holiness, but also that he is infinite, eternal, and unchangeable in his wisdom and in his justice, goodness, and truth.

Does that seem surprising to you in the light of what we have just been saying? Well, perhaps it might seem to be surprising. These qualities—wisdom, justice, goodness, and truth—are such startlingly human qualities. Can we ascribe them to that infinite, eternal, and unchangeable God of whom we have just been speaking? If we do try to ascribe them to that God, are we not guilty of a naïve anthropomorphism? Are we not guilty of the childish error of thinking of God as though he were just a big man up in the sky? Are we not guilty of making a god in our own image?

The answer is: no, we are not guilty of that. If we think of God as having some attributes which we also possess, we may conceivably be doing it for one or the other of two reasons. In the first place, we may be doing it because we are making God in our own image. But, in the second place, we may be doing it because God has made us in his image.

The Bible tells us that this second alternative is correct. God made man in the image of God, and that is the reason why God possesses some attributes which man also possesses, though God possesses them to an infinitely higher degree.

The Bible is not afraid of speaking of God in a startlingly tender and human sort of way. It does so just in passages where the majesty of God is set forth. "It is he who sits above the circle of the earth," says the fortieth chapter of Isaiah, "and its inhabitants are like grasshoppers" (Isa 40:22). "All the nations are as nothing before him, they are accounted by him as less than nothing and emptiness" (Isa 40:17). But what says that same fortieth chapter of Isaiah about this same terrible God? Here is what it says: "He will tend his flock like a shepherd; he will gather the lambs in his arms; he will carry them in his bosom, and gently lead those that are with young" (Isa 40:11).

How wonderfully the Bible sets forth the tenderness of God! Is that merely figurative? Are we wrong in thinking of God in such childlike fashion? Many philosophers say so. They will not think of God as a person. Oh, no. That would be dragging him down too much to our level! So they make of him a pale abstraction. The Bible seems childish to them in the warm, personal way in which it speaks of God.

Are those philosophers right or is the Bible right? Thank God, the Bible is right, my friends. The philosophers despise children who think of God as their heavenly Father. But the philosophers are wrong and the children are right. Did not our Lord Jesus say: "I thank you, Father, Lord of heaven and earth, that you have hidden these things from the wise and understanding and revealed them to little children" (Matt 11:25).

No, God is no pale abstraction. He is a person. That simple truth—precious possession of simple souls—is more profound than all the philosophies of all the ages.

But now we come to a great mystery. God, according to the Bible, is not just one person, but he is three persons in one God. That is the great mystery of the Trinity.

The Trinity is revealed to us only in the Bible. God has revealed some things to us through nature and through conscience. But the Trinity is not among them. This he has revealed to us by supernatural revelation and by supernatural revelation alone.

We can, it is true, detect something in the doctrine of the Trinity that serves to render clearer and richer even what nature and conscience reveal. Nature and conscience reveal—in a revelation which, it is true, sinful man seldom receives—a personal and holy God, Creator of the world. But how can a personal and holy being exist entirely alone? The thing is difficult for us to understand. That difficulty is wonderfully overcome by the doctrine of the Trinity, which tells us that even before God had created the world there was a personal inter-relation within the Godhead.

But we ought to be exceedingly cautious about such considerations. Though God is a person, he is a person very different from us finite persons, and I am not sure that we could ever have said, on the basis of any general revelation in nature and conscience, that an infinite person could not have existed entirely alone. Let us put such considerations, then, aside. When we are engaging in them we are venturing upon holy ground, where we can walk at best with but trembling and halting footsteps. The thing that is perfectly clear is that we should not have had any real knowledge of the holy mystery of the Trinity had not that mystery been revealed to us in the written Word of God.

Within the Word of God, it is in the New Testament that the doctrine of the Trinity is taught. There are hints of it in the Old Testament, but they are only hints, and it was left to the New Testament for this precious doctrine to be clearly revealed.

In the New Testament, the doctrine is taught with the utmost clearness; and the doctrine is presupposed even more than it is expressly taught, as has well been pointed out by Dr. B. B. Warfield in a splendid article, "The Biblical Doctrine of the Trinity." That is, the New Testament is founded throughout on the doctrine of the Trinity, and the doctrine was really established by the great facts of the incarnation of the Son of God and the work of the Holy Spirit even before it was enunciated in words.

Only the smallest part of the teaching of the New Testament about the Trinity is found in passages where the doctrine is stated as a whole. What the New Testament ordinarily does is to state parts of the doctrine, so that when we put those parts together, and when we summarize them, we have the great doctrine of the three persons and one God.

For example, all passages in the New Testament where the deity of Jesus Christ is set forth are, when taken in connection with passages setting forth the deity and personality of the Holy Spirit, passages supporting the doctrine of the Trinity. In the next talk, I hope to deal with some of those passages.

But what needs to be observed now is that although by far the larger part of the biblical teaching about the Trinity is given in that incidental and partial way—presupposing the doctrine rather than formally enunciating it as a whole—yet there are some passages where the doctrine is definitely presented by the mention, together, of Father, Son, and Holy Ghost.

The most famous of such passages, I suppose, is found in the Great Commission, given by the risen Lord to his disciples according to the twenty-eighth chapter of Matthew: "Go therefore and make disciples of all nations, baptizing them in the name of the Father and of the Son and of the Holy Spirit" (Matt 28:19).

There we have a mention of all three persons of the Trinity in the most complete coordination and equality—yet all three persons are plainly not three Gods but one. Here, in this solemn Commission by our Lord, the God of all true Christians is forever designated as a triune God.

We think also, for example, of the apostolic benediction at the end of the Second Epistle to the Corinthians: "The grace of the Lord Jesus Christ and the love of God and the fellowship of the Holy Spirit be with you all" (2 Cor 13:14). Here the terminology is a little different from that in the Great Commission. Paul speaks of the Son as "the Lord." But the word "Lord" in the Pauline epistles is plainly a designation of deity, like the other Greek word which is translated into English by the word "God." It is the Greek word used to translate the holy name of God, "Jehovah," in the Greek translation of the Old Testament which Paul used, and Paul does not hesitate to apply to Christ Old Testament passages which speak of Jehovah.

That brings us to something supremely important in the teaching of the whole New Testament about the Trinity. It is this: the New Testament writers, in presenting God as triune, are never for one moment conscious of saying anything that could by any possibility be regarded as contradicting the Old Testament teaching that there is but one God. That teaching is at the very heart and core of the Old Testament. It is every whit as much at the heart and core of the New Testament. The new Testament is just as much opposed as the Old Testament is to the thought that there are more Gods than one. Yet the New Testament with equal clearness teaches that the Father is God and the Son is God and the Holy Spirit is God, and that these three are not three aspects of the same person but three persons standing in a truly personal relationship to one another. There we have the great doctrine of the three persons but one God.

That doctrine is a mystery. No human mind can fathom it. Yet what a blessed mystery it is! The Christian's heart melts within him in gratitude and joy when he thinks of the divine love and condescension that has thus lifted the veil and allowed us sinful creatures a look into the very depths of the being of God.

TWO

What Is the Deity of Christ?

We have been talking about the great mystery of the Trinity. We have seen that according to the Bible there is one God in three persons—the Father, the Son, and the Holy Ghost. There are some places in the New Testament where all three persons of the Godhead are mentioned in the same verse. But much the more important or extensive part of the biblical proof of the doctrine of the Trinity is found in those passages where parts of the great doctrine are so mentioned as that when they are put together the completed doctrine inevitably appears. I want to begin to talk to you today about one great central part of the doctrine. I want to talk to you about the deity of our Lord Jesus Christ.

But before I can say a single word to you about the deity

of Christ, I must tell you what that term "the deity of Christ" means, or rather, I must make perfectly clear to you what it does not mean. I must make perfectly clear to you the fact that the term "deity of Christ" and the assertion "Jesus is God" are often so employed today as to mean something quite contrary to the Bible and to the Christian faith.

Do you not see, my friends, that when a man says he believes in the deity of Christ, or when he says he believes that Jesus is God, the significance of such assertions depends altogether upon the question what the man who makes them means by the term "deity" or the term "God."

If a man has a low view of deity, then, when he says that he believes in the deity of Christ, that means that he has a low view of Christ; and if he has a low view of God, then, when he says that he believes that Jesus is God, that means that he has a low view of Jesus.

But here is where the confusion comes in. A Christian man, hearing some unbeliever say that he believes in the deity of Christ or believes that Jesus is God, attributes to that unbeliever the *Christian* definition of the term "deity" or the term "God." He simply assumes that the term "deity" or the term "God" means what Christians have always taken those terms as meaning. That is, he assumes that those terms refer to a personal God, Creator and Ruler of the world, separate by a mighty gulf from all finite things. The consequence is that he is very much impressed when those terms are used about Jesus by a man who otherwise seemed to be very far from the Christian faith. "Did you not hear that man say," he exclaims, "that he believes in the deity of Christ; did you not hear him call Jesus 'God'? Well, if he believes in the deity of Christ, if he is willing to call Jesus 'God,' he cannot be so very wrong. He may be unorthodox in some particulars, but surely the root of the matter must be in him."

When I hear Christian people talking in that fashion about one of the noted unbelievers of the day, I have the sad feeling that those Christian people are, if I may use plain language, being deceived.

I am not a bit ashamed of laying stress upon this point, because I think it is a matter of profound importance. If I were sure I could get it really straight in your minds, I should think it worthwhile to devote not merely a part of one lecture to it, but a whole series of lectures. The more I look out upon the condition of the church, the more I am convinced that untold harm is being done by this double use of the term "deity" and of the term "God." The willingness of unbelievers to use the terms in *their* sense, coupled with the proneness of Christians to understand them in their own, is causing the great issue in the church between Christianity and unbelief to be obscured. What is the result? The result is that the church is being undermined from within. Christian people are being lulled to sleep by this use of orthodox terminology. Unbelievers are quietly gaining control. The young people of the church are being trained up in unbelief. Precious souls are being destroyed.

What ought we to do in such a situation? I will tell you what we ought to do, my friends. We ought to seek light, and we ought to pray God for light. We ought to pray God that people may cease to be satisfied by a word, but may insist on looking at the meaning of the word.

Now the Christian meaning of the term "deity of Christ" is fairly clear. The Christian believes that there is a personal God, Creator and Ruler of the universe, a God who is infinite, eternal, and unchangeable. So when the Christian says that Jesus Christ is God, or when he says that he believes in the deity of Christ, he means that that same person who is known to history as Jesus of Nazareth existed, before he became man, from all eternity as infinite, eternal, and unchangeable God, the second person of the holy Trinity.

Very different is the use of the term "deity of Christ" or the term "God," as it is applied to Jesus by many leaders in the modern church.

You can tell that they are using the term in some sense entirely different from the Christian sense because of the things that they say about Jesus in detail, or, more, because of the things that they will *not* say. They will not say that Jesus was born of a virgin. They will not say that he worked miracles. They will not say that the things that he said were always true; they will not say that he died as our substitute on the cross; they will not say that he rose from the tomb on the third day. Yet, they say, he was God.

When they say he was God, are they saying something orthodox? Is that orthodox assertion of theirs to be put to their credit over against the unorthodox assertions that they have made?

We answer: "No, a thousand times no!" When these men say that they believe in the deity of Christ or that they believe Jesus is God, that is not the most orthodox but the least orthodox thing that they say. It is an orthodox and a blessed thing to say that the Jesus of the Bible is God; but to say that this poor, deluded enthusiast of modern reconstruction is God is horrible blasphemy. How low these men must think of God if they can use his name in that way!

But in what sense do these men use the term "God" or the term "deity" when they apply it to the purely human Jesus— their purely human Jesus whom they have reconstructed after their rejection of the New Testament account?

Sometimes they mean by calling Jesus "God" merely that they try to enter into the same religious experience as the religious experience of those who in past generations called Jesus

God. In the creeds of the church, they say, Jesus is called God. We do not believe, they say, that he is God in the sense in which the authors of those creeds believed it. Shall we then cease to use the creeds? Not at all, they say. When the authors of the creeds called Jesus God, they were expressing in the language of their day a very precious experience which we also can share. So, they say, we can use the creeds still. We do not, of course, take them literally. But we can use them as expressions of the historic faith of the church. We can still hold to the underlying spiritual meaning of the doctrines that they contain—including the doctrine of the deity of Christ.

Such repetitions of the creeds and such professions of belief in the deity of Christ are doing untold harm in the church today. No doubt they are comforting to the men who practice them. I have sympathy with those men. To those men this use of traditional terminology seems like the stained glass in an old cathedral. It puts everything in a sort of dim religious light; it seems to impart a solemn glow of sanctity to what would appear to be bald unbelief if it were viewed in the cruel light of day.

But the trouble is that ordinary people in the church are being deceived. They hear a man repeating the creeds. He seems to be repeating them with the utmost fervor. He is particularly fervent in expressing his belief in the deity of Christ. They simply assume that he means by the deity of Christ what people have always meant by it. So they tolerate him in the church and put him in a position of authority. Time goes on. Many such men are put into positions of greater and greater authority. They undermine the faith of the church, partly by their words, but more particularly by their silence. A deadly vagueness gradually affects the church's witness. The young people of the church are not soundly indoctrinated. People do not know what is wrong, but the church loses its power. Finally, the mask is thrown off. The people who really believe in the Bible and in the creed of the church and who are dead in earnest about that belief are treated as troublemakers. The church sinks down into a merger with the world.

That has been the process in many churches of our day. But it is not in that way that we believe in the deity of Christ. When we say we believe in the deity of Christ, when we repeat the great creeds, we are not just using a form of words that meant something to somebody of long ago. No, we are saying something that we do honestly hold ourselves to be true. We are not just giving expression to the historic faith of the church, but we are giving expression to *our* faith. We are saying that the historic faith of the church is what we ourselves believe.

But aside from a merely traditional use of ancient terms, what is the actual meaning attributed to the terms "deity" and

"God" by those who have given up the meaning that is found in the Bible and in the great creeds of the church? What do modern unbelievers mean by speaking of the "deity of Christ" and what do they mean by calling Jesus "God"?

I think a twofold answer will have to be given to that question. Unbelievers who use the term "deity of Christ" and the term "God" as applied to Jesus mean usually one or the other of two things by those terms.

In the first place, some of them use the terms in what may be called a pantheizing sense. That is, they are willing to call Jesus "God" because they hold that all of us are God. They put only a difference of degree and not a difference of kind between Jesus's deity and ours. God, they say, is not a far-off God. His life pulsates through the life of all the world. He has always been incarnating himself in men and women. At one point he incarnated himself with particular fullness—namely, in Jesus of Nazareth. But that incarnation was not different in kind from the incarnation in other men. It was different in degree but not in kind. What is revealed by the appearance of such a man as Jesus on the earth is that God and man are essentially one.

It is needless to say that that view of the deity of Christ is just about the diametrical opposite of the Christian view, which the Bible teaches. According to the Bible, what is revealed by the appearance of Jesus upon the earth is not that God and man are one, but rather that God and man are not one. God is God and man is man. There can be no confusion between the two. Moreover, man is separate from God by the awful abyss of sin. Hence—just because of that separation between God and man—the eternal Son of God, second person of the holy Trinity, took upon himself our nature, by an act that was done not many times but once and once only, and so because of that one act "was, and continueth to be God, and man, in two distinct natures, and one person, forever" (WSC Q&A 21).

I am not going to try to speak today of the relation between the divine nature and the human nature in the person of Christ. That belongs to a later talk in this series. But what I want now to do is simply to say that the words, "Jesus is God," have no real meaning, certainly no biblical or Christian meaning, unless they go with the supplementary belief that *we* most emphatically are *not* God.

In the second place, other unbelievers use the terms "deity of Christ" or the term "God" as applied to Jesus in what may be called an anti-metaphysical or positivistic sense. I trust you have some spirit left in you when I use words as long as those. I do not expect all of you to understand the word "positivistic" right at the start, but I do hope to make you understand the thing that I mean by that word. I mean to designate by it the view of people who regard the human life of the man Jesus as the only God that they know. People used to believe, they say, that there is a personal God, Creator and Ruler of the world. But we no longer believe that—at least we are quite uncertain about it. It belongs to the realm of metaphysics, which is a very doubtful realm. The only things that we can be really certain about are the things that we can see and hear, the things that are found here in this world in which we live. So if we are to have a God, a modern God, we must find him here in the midst of us—here in this plainly visible realm.

Now we want to find a God, say the men of this way of thinking. People who used to believe in that old metaphysical God, Maker and Ruler of the universe, had something that we are in danger of losing. They had religion. They had a Being who could call forth ennobling emotions of reverence and awe. We need those emotions. We need something to call them forth. We need something to worship.

Where shall we find something to call forth these emotions? Were shall we find something to worship? Where shall we find an adequate object of religious devotion to take the place of that personal Creator in whom we no longer believe? We must find it here upon this earth, say these people of whom we are now speaking. Where then shall we find it?

Why, we find it, they say, in the life of a certain man named Jesus. He was not, of course, the Creator of the world. He was a man like the rest of men. But his moral life can call forth the same reverence as past generations used to give to the supposed Creator of the world. So although metaphysics is gone, religion remains. Men used to have the ennobling emotion of reverence as they turned to the starry heavens and said: "The heavens declare the glory of God, and the sky above proclaims his handiwork" (Ps 19:1). We no longer believe all that. But we can experience those same ennobling emotions by contemplating the human life of the man Jesus.

Such is a very common view of what men call "the deity of Christ." What shall we say about that view? What shall we say about that way of worshiping Jesus? I will tell you what I think we ought to say about it. I think we ought to say about it that it is a terrible sin.

Please do not misunderstand me. It is not a sin to worship Jesus. On the contrary, it is the highest and noblest privilege and duty ever given to man. It is not a sin to worship the real Jesus. It is not a sin to worship the Jesus who is God and man. But it is a sin to manufacture a Jesus who was man only and not God, and then after you have manufactured that purely human Jesus to bow down and worship him.

Do you not see what that kind of worship of the moral life of a supposedly purely human Jesus, a Jesus who is regarded merely as the ideal man—do you not see what that worship of such a purely human Jesus really means? It means that the man who engages in it has committed the ancient and terrible sin of worshiping humanity. It means that he has worshiped and served the creature rather than the Creator, and that is a sin indeed.

The upshot of what I have been saying is this: when men today say that Christ is God they often do so not because they think high of Christ but because they think desperately low of God.

That is not at all the way in which the Bible says that Christ is God. When the Bible says that Christ is God, it does not do that by dragging God down. It does not ask us to forget a single thing that it has said about the stupendous majesty of God. No, it asks us to remember every one of those things in order that we may apply them all to Jesus Christ.

The Bible tells us in the first verse that God in the beginning created the heavens and the earth. Does it ask us to forget that when it tells us that Jesus Christ is God? No, it asks us to remember that. It says of Jesus Christ: "All things were made through him, and without him was not any thing made that was made" (John 1:3).

The Bible tells us that God is infinite, eternal, and unchangeable. Does it ask us to forget that when it tells us that Christ is God? No, it tells us to remember that. "I am the Alpha and the Omega," says Christ, "the first and the last, the beginning and the end" (Rev 22:13). "Before Abraham was, I am" (John 8:58). "In the beginning was the Word" (John 1:1). "He is before all things, and in him all things hold together" (Col 1:17).

The Bible tells us that God is holy. Does it ask us to forget that when it tells us that Christ is God? Let the whole New Testament give the answer.

The Bible tells us that God is mysterious. Does it ask us to forget that when it tells us that Christ is God? No, it tells us that there are mysteries in Christ which only God can know. No one knoweth the Son but the Father, says Jesus, as no one knoweth the Father but the Son (see Matt 11:27; Luke 10:22).

The Bible tells us that God is the final judge. Does it ask us to forget that when it tells us that Jesus is God? No, Jesus himself said, in the Sermon on the Mount, that he would sit upon the judgment throne to judge all the earth.

Everywhere it is the same, my friends. The Bible from Genesis to Revelation presents a stupendous view of God, and then it tells us that Jesus Christ is all that God is.

What interest has the Christian man in all that? What interest has the Christian man in knowing that Jesus Christ is very God, what interest in knowing that it was through him that the worlds were made, what interest in knowing that he pervades the remotest bounds, what interest in knowing that he is infinite in knowledge and in power?

No interest, say modern unbelievers; these things are mere metaphysics.

Every interest, say Christians; these things are the very breath of our lives.

We have trusted in Jesus. But how far can we trust him? Just in this transitory life? Just in this little speck that we call the earth? If we can trust him only thus far we are of all men most miserable. We are surrounded by stupendous forces; we are surrounded by the immensity of the unknown. After our little span of life there is a shelving brink with the infinite beyond. And still we are subject to fear—not only fear of destruction but a more dreadful fear of meeting with the infinite and holy God.

So we should be if we had but a human Christ. But now is Christ our Savior, the one who says, "Your sins are forgiven," revealed as very God. And we believe. Such a faith is a mystery to us who possess it; it seems folly to those who have it not. But if possessed it delivers us forever from fear. The world to us is all unknown; it is engulfed in an ocean of infinity. But it contains no mysteries to our Savior. He is on the throne. He pervades the remotest bounds. He inhabits infinity. With such a Savior we are safe.

THREE

Does the Bible Teach the Deity of Christ?

In the last talk I began to speak about the deity of Christ. But I had to point out the disconcerting fact that in contemporary parlance the term "deity of Christ" and the term "God" as applied to Jesus mean practically nothing. They are used in so many different senses that the use of these terms has in itself lost all significance. Unbelievers who have a very low view of Jesus indeed are perfectly willing to say that Jesus is God. They are willing to say that Jesus is God not because they have a high view of Jesus but because they have a low view of God.

It is a relief to turn from such intellectual quagmires, where words no longer mean what they say, to the Bible. In modern parlance, with its boundless degradation of formerly lofty terms, there is no solid footing; but it is not so in the Bible. The Bible defines its terms with the utmost clearness, and therefore when the Bible says that Jesus is God, we readers of the Bible know exactly where we stand.

Just now, therefore, we have a much pleasanter task than that which we had in the last talk. We are going to try to begin to set forth in positive fashion a little bit at least of what the Bible says about the deity of Christ.

If we are going to do so with any completeness we should have to begin with the Old Testament. It is true, the Old Testament does not set forth the doctrine of the deity of Christ with any fullness. I do not suppose that either the prophets or their hearers knew in any clear fashion that the coming Messiah was to be one of the persons in the Godhead. Yet there are wonderful intimations of the doctrine of the deity of Christ even in the Old Testament. The outstanding fact is that the hope of a coming Messiah, as it appears with increasing clearness in the Old Testament books, goes far beyond any mere expectations of an earthly king of David's line. The Messiah, according to the Old Testament, is clearly to be a supernatural person, and he is clearly possessed of attributes that are truly divine.

It has often been observed that before the time of Christ, there were two types of Messianic expectation among the Jews. According to one type, the Messiah was to be a king of David's line; according to the other, he was to be a heavenly being suddenly appearing in the clouds of heaven to judge the world.

Both of these types of later Jewish expectation are rooted in the Old Testament. The Old Testament represents the Messiah both as a king of David's line and also as a supernatural person to appear with the clouds of heaven. The former of these two representations appears, for example, in the seventh chapter of Second Samuel, where a never-ending line of kings to be descended from David is promised; and it appears even more clearly in the passages where the coming of one supreme king of David's line is promised. The latter of the two representations appears, for example, in the seventh chapter of Daniel, where a mysterious person "like a son of man" is seen, in the prophet's vision, in the presence of the "Ancient of Days"—a mysterious person to whom is given a universal and everlasting dominion (Dan 7:13).

These two types of Messianic expectation in the Old Testament are by no means sharply distinguished from one another. When we examine closely the expected king of David's line, we find that he is to be far more than an ordinary earthly king; we find that he has distinctly supernatural attributes: and, on the other hand, the supernatural figure of the seventh chapter of Daniel is by no means separate from Israel but appears as the representative of the Old Testament people of God.

This possession of both divine and human attributes by the Messiah appears with particular clearness in the ninth chapter of Isaiah. There the coming deliverer is spoken of as one who shall sit upon the throne of David. Yet his kingdom is to be everlasting, and he himself is actually called "Mighty God, Everlasting Father, Prince of Peace" (Isa 9:6). There we have the deity of the coming Messiah presented in the Old Testament in so many words.

Now the glorious thing is that in the New Testament we find these two types of Old Testament promise about the Messiah united, in the fulfilment, in the same person. How is it that one person can on the one hand be a man, a king of David's line, and at the same time be the mighty God? The question is not fully answered in the Old Testament. But the New Testament answers it most wonderfully in the great central doctrine of the two natures in the one person of our Lord. Yes, the coming deliverer was indeed to be both mighty God and a king of David's line, because the mighty God in strange condescension and love became man for our sakes "and so was, and continueth to be God, and man, in two distinct natures, and one person, forever" (WSC Q&A 21).

But we are not now speaking about the relation between the divine nature and the human nature in Christ. What we are now interested in saying is that the Old Testament does teach the deity of the coming Messiah. Here, as at so many other points, there is a wonderful continuity between the Old Testament and the New.

The continuity is fully recognized by the New Testament. The New Testament does not present the doctrine of the Trinity, including the doctrine of the deity of Christ, as though it meant the introduction of a new idea of God. On the contrary, it presents it as being a revelation of the same God as the God who had revealed himself to Israel in Old Testament times. That is finely brought out in the article on the Trinity by B. B. Warfield, to which we have already referred. The Jehovah of the Old Testament is presented in the New Testament as being a triune God; but he is the same God throughout both the Old Testament and the New.

Hence it is only what is to be expected when we find that the New Testament applies to Christ Old Testament passages where the God of Israel is called by his holiest and most precious name, "Jehovah." Could there be any clearer testimony to the full deity of Jesus Christ?

Dr. Warfield rightly calls attention also to the matter-of-course way in which this identity of the triune God of the New Testament with the covenant God of Israel appears in the New Testament books. The New Testament writers are apparently not conscious of saying anything revolutionary. They assume the doctrine of the deity of Christ more than they expressly teach it. Why do they assume it? Dr. Warfield gives the answer. They assume it because it had already been established by the fact of the coming of the Son of God in the flesh. The doctrine was established by the fact of the incarnation before it was set forth in words. When the eternal Son of God became man in order to redeem sinners on the cross, and when the Holy Spirit was sent to apply that redeeming work of the Son of God to those who should be saved, then the doctrine of the Trinity was made known to men. The church from the very beginning was founded upon that doctrine; it was the factual revelation of that doctrine by the coming of the Son and the coming of the Spirit that ushered in the new dispensation.

However, although it was the factual revelation of the doctrine which in a true sense came first, yet the doctrine is taught also in words, and taught in the plainest possible way. In setting forth the way in which it is taught, one great difficulty is the difficulty of selection. The whole New Testament teaches the deity of Christ, and that is what makes it hard for us to decide what individual passages we shall mention. Where the store is so very rich, it is hard to make a selection from it.

Let us begin with the point of time at which the New Testament narrative begins. Let us begin with the annunciation of the birth of John the Baptist, as it is recorded in the first chapter of Luke. The angel promises to Zacharias that he will have a son, who will, in accordance with the prophecy in Malachi, go before the Lord to make ready his people for him (Luke 1:16–80).

There is here no clear reference to the Messiah as a distinct person. The promised son of Zacharias is to go before Jehovah, or, in the Greek form, "the Lord"; but it is not said that he is to go before the Messiah. Yet there is no doubt but that the author of the Gospel according to Luke, when he quotes the angel's words, identifies that coming of Jehovah with which the Malachi prophecy dealt and to which the angel alludes with the coming of Jesus Christ. The coming of Jehovah is the coming of Christ. There is also no doubt but that in making that identification the author of this Gospel is in accordance with the whole New Testament and in accordance with the real meaning of what the angel said. We have here just one instance of that stupendous fact of which we have already spoken—the fact that the New Testament writers apply to Jesus things that the Old Testament says of Jehovah. The whole New Testament is based upon the thought that there is some strange essential unity between Jesus Christ and the covenant God of Israel.

Then we have the annunciation of the angel to the virgin Mary (Luke 1:30–38). The annunciation is partly in Old Testament terms. Mary's son is to sit on the throne of David; and when it is said that of his kingdom there is to be no end, that also does not go beyond what the Old Testament had promised about the Messiah. But then a great mystery is revealed. The promised child is not to have a human father by ordinary generation, but is to be conceived by the Holy Ghost in the womb of a virgin mother. Even that—at least the part of it that sets forth the fact that the mother is to be a virgin—is found in Old Testament prophecy (in Isa 7:14)—but that prophecy had not been understood among the Jews. Now, just before the fulfillment, the prophecy is repeated in fuller and more glorious terms. The conception of this child in the womb of the virgin Mary is to be a miracle wrought by the immediate power of the Spirit of God. That miracle is one of the things that will show the child to be rightly called "holy" and "Son of God."

Evidently the term "Son of God" is here used in some very lofty sense. It does not designate the promised child merely as the Messiah, though sometimes the Messiah was called "Son of God." Evidently the term is used here in some unique and stupendous sense.

At twelve years of age, the child Jesus was found in the temple. Joseph and Mary had sought him sorrowing, and at last they found him among the doctors, hearing them and asking them questions. "Son," Mary said, "why have you treated us so? Behold, your father and I have been searching for you in great distress." Then came the strange answer of the boy Jesus: "Did you not know that I must be in my Father's house?" (Luke 2:48–49). When Mary spoke of the father of that twelve-year-old boy, she meant his human father, the one who stood to him in a relation more like that of a father than did any other human being. When the boy Jesus spoke of his Father in reply, he meant God. Notice that he did not say, "our Father," when he spoke of God. No, he said, "my Father." He was Son of God in a sense entirely different from that which would apply to any other person who ever lived upon this earth.

That brings us to one of the strangest things about the way in which Jesus all through the Gospels speaks of God. This strange thing appears not only in the Gospel according to John, which modern unbelief rejects so radically as untrue, but also in the Synoptic Gospels. The strange thing is that Jesus according to all four of the Gospels never speaks of God as "our Father," classing himself with his disciples in that word "our." He says, "my Father," and he says to his disciples, "your Father," but never does he say, "our Father," classing himself with his disciples in that filial relationship to God. The Lord's Prayer begins with those words "our Father," but Jesus certainly did not pray that prayer with his disciples, because that prayer contains a confession of sin, and Jesus never had any sin to confess. It was a prayer that he taught his disciples, not a prayer that he prayed himself. The significant fact remains, therefore. Jesus never appears in the Gospels as saying "Our Father" to God together with his disciples. God was his Father, and God was their Father; but he was his Father in an entirely different sense from the sense in which he was their Father. Jesus was Son of God in an entirely unique way.

At the beginning of the Gospel according to Mark, with the parallel passages in Matthew and Luke, we are told about the beginning of Jesus's public ministry. That event was marked by a miracle. The Spirit descended upon Jesus, and there was a voice from heaven that said: "You are my beloved Son; with you I am well pleased" (Mark 1:11). It is possible that the good pleasure of God which is here spoken of is the definite act of approval accomplished at the moment when Jesus was sent forth into his public ministry. Yet, even so, that divine act of approval is evidently regarded as rooted in a unique relationship in which the person thus approved had always stood toward God. Jesus did not become Son of God because he had divine approval, but he had that divine approval because he had always been Son of God.

For a further discussion of that question and similar questions? I may refer you incidentally to the learned and most illuminating book on *The Self-Disclosure of Jesus*, by Geerhardus Vos.

At any rate, Jesus now comes forward in his public ministry. In what light does he present himself in that public ministry?

Here one great central fact stares us in the face. I think it would hardly be possible to lay too much stress upon it. It is this: Jesus does not present himself merely as an example for faith but presents himself as the object of faith. That fact appears not merely in the Gospel according to John, which unbelievers reject as altogether unhistorical; but it appears also in the three Synoptic Gospels, and in the Synoptic Gospels it appears even in those parts which are supposed by modern criticism, rightly or wrongly, to come from the earliest sources underlying the Gospels. You cannot get away from it anywhere in the Gospels. It is all-pervasive. That fact has been demonstrated in particularly convincing fashion by James Denney in his book *Jesus and the Gospel.* I do not commend that book to you in general. In some respects it is a sadly mistaken book. But it does show in a singularly convincing way that everywhere in the New Testament, including the Synoptic Gospels, and including the sources supposed rightly or wrongly to underlie the Synoptic Gospels, Jesus is represented not as a mere example for faith but as the object of faith.

What do we mean by saying that? What do we mean by saying that Jesus is presented not primarily as an example for faith but as the object of faith? We mean something very simple and at the same time something very stupendous. We mean that Jesus did not come forward merely saying: "Look at me; I am practicing the true religion, and I bid you practice the same religion as that which I am practicing." We mean that he did not come forward merely saying: "Look at me; I have faith in God, and I bid you have faith in God like my faith in God." We mean that he did not come forward merely saying: "Look at me; I regard God as my Father, and I bid you to regard God as your Father too in the same sense as that in which I regard him as my Father."

It is so that modern unbelievers represent Jesus. They regard him as a guide out into a larger type of religious life. They regard him as being the founder of Christianity because he was the first Christian. They regard Christianity as consisting in imitation of the religious life of Jesus. So they love to speak of "the religion of Jesus"; they love to speak of the gospel *of* Jesus in distinction from a gospel *about* Jesus. Thus they degrade Jesus to the position of a mere teacher and example. They turn away from the gospel that has him as its substance to a gospel which was merely the gospel that he preached.

When they do that, it is evident that they are turning away from what has been known as Christianity for the past nineteen hundred years. But they are also turning away from Jesus himself as he is presented to us in all the sources of historical information that we know anything about. According to all the four Gospels, and according to all the supposed sources which modern criticism has tried to detect back of the four Gospels, Jesus put himself into his gospel; the gospel *of* Jesus was also a gospel *about* Jesus; the gospel that he preached was also a gospel that offered him as Savior. He did not say merely: "Have faith in God like the faith that I have in God," but he said: "Have faith *in me*."

That appears of course with the utmost clearness in the Gospel according to John. But it also appears in the Synoptic Gospels. There was, indeed, according to the Synoptic Gospels, a period in the public ministry of Jesus when he did not ordinarily make his own person the express subject of systematic discourse. But if you look a little deeper, you see that everywhere Jesus was offering himself as the Savior of men and asking them to have faith in him.

That appears, for example, in his miracles of healing. "Your faith has saved you," he says, "go in peace" (Luke 7:50). Well, faith in whom? Perhaps we might be tempted to say merely, "Faith in God like the faith which Jesus had in God." But I bid you read the narratives with care and ask yourselves whether that interpretation really does justice to them. I think you will find that it does not. No, Jesus was presenting himself when he worked those miracles as one in whom he was bidding men have confidence. No doubt he was bidding them have confidence in God the Father. But the point is that that confidence in God the Father was also confidence in him. The faith that saved those people was faith in Jesus Christ.

He was saving those people from bodily ills, but he was also saving their souls from sin. That becomes explicit in the healing of the paralytic borne of four, where Jesus says not only, "Rise and walk," but "Your sins are forgiven you" (Luke 5:23 and parallels). But it is really implied in the cases where it is not expressed. Jesus, according to all the Gospels, saves men from sin, and the means which he uses to save them from sin is the faith which he bids them have in him, the Savior.

Thus Jesus, according to all the Gospels, presents himself as the object of a truly religious faith. Well, who is the object of a truly religious faith? The answer is very simple. He is God. The way in which Jesus presents himself as the object of faith in all the Gospels—and even in the sources supposed, rightly or wrongly, to underlie the Gospels—is a tremendous testimony by Jesus himself to his own deity. That testimony does not appear merely in individual passages. It is a kind of atmosphere that pervades the whole picture, or, to change the figure, a foundation that sustains the whole building. If you ignore it, the whole account which the Bible gives of Jesus becomes a hopeless puzzle.

In the next talk, I want to continue to deal with the deity of Christ. Today I have been able to do no more than make a beginning in the presentation of that great subject. I wonder what you think about it. What do you think of Jesus Christ? Do you think of him, with modern unbelievers, merely as the initiator of a higher type of religious life, the discoverer of certain permanent facts about the fatherhood of God and the brotherhood of man? Or do you think of him, as Christians do, as the Lord of glory, the eternal Son of God become man to save you from your sins?

Or, finally, are you undecided with regard to him? Are you undecided which of these two views you will hold? Do you belong to that great army of persons who stand outside the household of faith and look longingly at the warmth and joy within? Are you hindered from entering in by gloomy doubts? If you belong to that third class, we pray God that you may be led to say at least: "I believe; help my unbelief" (Mark 9:24). If you do say that, the Lord will help your unbelief, as he helped the man who said that so long ago, and will bring you into the clear shining of faith.

FOUR

The Sermon
on the Mount

We are now in the midst of our discussion of the great
theme, the deity of Jesus Christ. Was Jesus a mere man,
a leader into a higher and better type of religious experience, or
was he the eternal Son of God become man to save us from the
guilt and power of sin?

We have already begun to point out what the Bible says
about this question. In particular, we have pointed out that all
four of the Gospels, and even the sources supposed, rightly or
wrongly, to underlie the Gospels, represent Jesus not merely as
an example of faith but as the object of faith—that is, they represent Jesus not as saying merely, "Have faith in God like the
faith which I have in God," but as saying, "Have faith in me."
But that means that the four Gospels teach the deity of Christ

and represent Jesus himself as teaching it. The object of a truly religious faith is none other than God.

I want now to show you how extraordinarily pervasive in the Gospels is the lofty view of Jesus Christ which necessarily goes with his offer of himself as the object of faith. People try to escape from that lofty view of Christ. They like to regard Jesus just as a teacher and example; they say that this whole notion about his deity is an unfortunate metaphysical notion that has nothing to do with vital religion. Let us get away from metaphysics and theology, they say, and, instead, just get up and obey Jesus's commands; if we obey his commands we are honoring him more than we could honor him by any amount of intellectual convictions regarding his deity.

Well, my friend, I will say to a man of this way of thinking, where will you turn in the Gospels to get away from a lofty view of the person of Christ; where will you turn to find a Jesus who simply gave men directions for the ordering of their lives and did not demand that they should have any particular view about him? Here is a New Testament, my friend; will you just open it anywhere you like in order to prove your point?

I suppose that if I should say that to one of the advocates of this non-doctrinal Christianity, he would be most apt to turn, among all the passages in the New Testament, to the Sermon on the Mount. In the Sermon on the Mount, it is often said, we have a program for Christian living that is quite independent of the niceties of orthodox theology, and if we should just be willing to live that kind of life it would be a great deal better than disputing about theological questions or even being too anxious to get a completely orthodox notion about Jesus himself.

Well, my friend, you have turned to the Sermon on the Mount. I did not choose it. You chose it. It is your favorite passage. You cannot object, therefore, if we examine it a little for ourselves to see whether it really teaches that kind of non-doctrinal religion that you so enthusiastically advocate. In particular, you cannot object if we examine it to see whether it is really silent about those stupendous claims of Jesus which so trouble you in other parts of the New Testament.

All right, then; we are going to put preconceived opinions aside and examine the Sermon on the Mount for ourselves.

What happens to us when we do that? I will tell you very plainly. We find that the Sermon on the Mount teaches and presupposes that same stupendous view of Jesus Christ which underlies all the rest of the Gospels.

The Sermon on the Mount (see Matt 5:1ff) might seem to begin in a way unfavorable to that view and favorable to the advocate of a non-doctrinal Christianity who is not interested in the question what sort of person Jesus is. It begins with the Beatitudes, and the Beatitudes might seem at first sight to be independent of any particular view regarding the one who spoke them. "Blessed are the poor in spirit, for theirs is the kingdom of heaven"—does not that remain true whatever we think of the person who uttered it?

Well, I am not sure even about that. I am not sure but that in all of the Beatitudes we detect a strange note of authority which would be overwrought and pathological in any other person than the Jesus of the Bible. Who is this who tells with such extraordinary assurance what sort of persons will be in the kingdom of God? Who is this that announces to men rewards that only God can give?

But let that pass for the moment. The thing that is clear is that Jesus does not finish the Beatitudes before he comes to speak in the most stupendous way about himself. What is the last of the Beatitudes? Is it merely a blessing pronounced upon people who possess a certain quality of soul? Not at all. It is a blessing pronounced upon people who stand in a certain relation to Jesus himself. Here is what it is: "Blessed are you when others revile you and persecute you and utter all kinds of evil against you falsely on my account" (Matt 5:11). Notice those words "on my account." They contain a tremendous claim on the part of Jesus. Men are to be willing to bear his name, and if they are not ashamed to bear his name they are to stand in the final judgment. Imagine any mere man saying that! Imagine anyone other than

Jesus saying: "Blessed are you if you suffer on account of me." We have here the words of the same Jesus as was the one who said: "If anyone comes to me and does not hate his own father and mother and wife and children and brothers and sisters, yes, and even his own life, he cannot be my disciple" (Luke 14:26), the same Jesus as the one who said: "For whoever is ashamed of me and of my words in this adulterous and sinful generation, of him will the Son of Man also be ashamed when he comes in the glory of his Father with the holy angels" (Mark 8:38). Who can claim such an exclusive devotion as that—a devotion which shall take precedence over even the holiest of earthly ties, a devotion upon which a man's eternal destiny depends? God can, but can any mere man?

Then comes that great section of the Sermon on the Mount where Jesus declares himself to have come not to destroy the law or the prophets but to fulfil. "You have heard that it was said to those of old," he says, and then makes several quotations. Those quotations contain in part sentences found in the Old Testament. Over against those quotations, Jesus in every case puts something of his own: "You have heard that it was said . . . but I say to you" (Matt 5:21ff). No doubt it may be held that Jesus in none of these instances is setting what he says over against what the Old Testament says, but in every instance is merely setting what he says over against what the

Jewish teachers had wrongly held that the Old Testament said. But even then the fact remains that what he sets forth against the wrong interpretation of the Old Testament passages is not just a right interpretation but something wonderfully fresh and new. Plainly Jesus puts his own sayings here on a level with the Old Testament pronouncements which he certainly regarded as the very Word of God.

I ask you to consider for a moment that authority with which Jesus speaks, that authority which causes him to put his own pronouncements fully on a level with the Old Testament pronouncements. What is the nature of that authority which Jesus here claims?

Well, prophets claimed authority. They asked that people should receive what they said as a message from God. Was then the authority which Jesus is here claiming merely the authority of a prophet? No, most emphatically it was not merely that. The prophets spoke with a divine authority. But it was a delegated authority, and it was delegated to them in a temporary way. There were times when the prophets became spokesmen of God, but they were spokesmen of God merely because they became for the moment channels for the Holy Spirit. They were not in general infallible. They had no authority which was granted them as a permanent possession to be used as they saw fit. When they came forward as prophets they were careful to give all honor to God.

Thus the characteristic way in which the prophets introduced their utterances was with the words, "Thus says the Lord." By that they meant to say: "I am not saying this as my own word, but it is God who is saying it; I am merely the mouthpiece of God."

Now unquestionably Jesus was a prophet. Undoubtedly the catechism that I learned in childhood was right when it told me that he was a prophet as well as a priest and a king.

But although Jesus was a prophet, he was also vastly more than a prophet. So he does not introduce these utterances of his in the Sermon on the Mount in the way in which the utterances of a prophet are introduced. He does not say, "Thus says the Lord." No, he says, "I say." He comes forward with his own authority, and that authority he places fully on a level with the authority of God as it was found expressed in the Old Testament.

I am not forgetting the places in the Gospels where the dependence of the man Jesus upon God is set forth. Those passages are found particularly just in the Gospel according to John—just in that Gospel where the deity of Christ is set forth, I will not say more clearly (since it is set forth with the utmost clearness in all the Gospels), but more expressly and fully, than in the other Gospels. Jesus, according to the Gospel of John, did what he saw God doing, and he said what God told him to say. All the same, despite this subordination of the man Jesus to God, his authority went far beyond the authority of a prophet. It was an authority which was his own personal right, as belonging to the one who was not merely man but God. You can search all through the words of the prophets and not find anything in the remotest degree resembling that stupendous "I say to you" of the Sermon on the Mount.

Then I bid you read on to the end of that Sermon on the Mount. "Not everyone" says Jesus, "who says to me, 'Lord, Lord,' will enter the kingdom of heaven, but the one who does the will of my Father who is in heaven" (Matt 7:21). That is one of the favorite texts of unbelievers. If the whole Sermon on the Mount is their favorite passage, this perhaps, within the Sermon on the Mount, may be regarded as their favorite text.

It is a favorite text with unbelievers not because of its real meaning, but because of the meaning which they wrongly attribute to it. They take it as meaning that if a man is what the world calls a good moral man then he will enter into the kingdom of God no matter what his attitude toward Jesus may be. But of course that is not what the text says. The text does not say that if a man does the will of God he will enter into the kingdom of God whether he says "Lord, Lord" to Jesus or not. It does not say that any man who does *not* say "Lord, Lord" to Jesus will enter into the kingdom. But what it does say is that even among those who say "Lord, Lord" to Jesus there are some who will not enter in. Those are the ones who say "Lord, Lord" only with their lips and not with their hearts, and who show that they have not said it with their hearts because they do not say it with their lives.

However, though for bad reasons, it is a popular text among unbelievers. They ought then to be willing to examine carefully what it says, and we all ought to examine it with them.

When we do examine it, we discover that it involves the most stupendous claim on the part of Jesus. For one thing, it provides an instance of the strange way in which Jesus speaks of God as being his own Father. "Not everyone who says to me, 'Lord, Lord,' will enter the kingdom of heaven," he says, "but the one who does the will of my Father who is in heaven." "*My* Father," says Jesus, not "*our* Father" or "*the* Father." We spoke of that in the talk just preceding this one. We noticed how it appeared in the answer of the twelve-year-old Jesus in the temple, and how it runs all through the Gospels. Well, here it is, in the Sermon on the Mount. You cannot get away from it. We do not particularly notice it as we read this verse, because we have become so used to it. But that does not destroy its tremendous significance. Indeed, it vastly increases it. Everywhere Jesus thinks of himself as being Son of God in some entirely unique sense.

But now let us look at what this verse itself says. We must take it in connection with the following two verses. Those verses also are favorites with the unbelievers of our day. They read as follows:

> On that day many will say to me, "Lord, Lord, did
> we not prophesy in your name, and cast out demons
> in your name, and do many mighty works in your
> name?" And then will I declare to them, "I never knew
> you; depart from me, you workers of lawlessness."
> (Matt 7:22–23)

Unbelievers, I suppose, interpret those words as disparaging miracles, and as disparaging the active profession of religion. They interpret them as teaching that if a man leads what the world calls a moral life he does not need to accept any creed or make any definite profession of faith.

That interpretation is of course quite wrong, in the same way as that in which the corresponding interpretation of the preceding verse is wrong. These verses do not say that miracles were unimportant in the apostolic age (when miracles still happened) or that orthodoxy was unimportant then or is unimportant now. They only say that nothing else matters unless a man's heart is changed and unless that change of his heart is shown in a good life. They do not say that orthodoxy is unnecessary or that mighty works in the external world are unimportant, but they only say that orthodoxy without right living is a sham, and that real orthodoxy results in obedience to the commands of God.

But the fact remains that these verses are favorites with unbelievers; they are favorites with those who think that it does not make any difference what a man thinks about God or about Christ and that all that is needed according to Jesus is to live what is ordinarily called a moral life.

All right. Let us just look at these verses so popular among unbelievers. Do they really teach that it does not make any difference what a man thinks about Jesus Christ? I tell you, my friends, the exact reverse is the case. These verses, like all the rest of the New Testament, present a stupendous view of Jesus Christ, and like other sayings of Jesus they present a stupendous claim made by Jesus himself.

What is the scene to which we are transplanted in these verses? Is it some scene in the course of ordinary history or some scene of merely local or temporary significance? No, it is nothing of the kind. It is the tremendous scene of the last judgment, the court from which there is no appeal, the final decision that determines the eternal destinies of men.

In other words, it is the judgment-seat of God. Well, who is it that is represented here as sitting on the judgment-seat of God; who is it that is represented here in this supposedly pleasant, purely ethical, practical, ultra-modern, non-theological

Sermon on the Mount, and by this supposedly simple teacher of righteousness who kept his own person out of his message and was careful not to advance any lofty claims—who is it that is represented here in this supposedly purely ethical discourse and by this humble Jesus as sitting one day upon the judgment-seat of God and as determining the eternal destinies of all the world? There can be no doubt whatever about the answer to that question. The one represented here as sitting on the judgment-seat of God is Jesus himself.

We may not like the answer to that question, but the answer is as plain as plain can be. "Many will say to *me*," Jesus says, "'Lord, Lord' . . . and then will I declare to them, 'I never knew you; depart from me, you workers of lawlessness.'" Who is that "I," and who is that "me"? Is it God the Father? No, it is Jesus; it is the one who speaks these words. Upon Jesus's decision depends the fate of all men. And what is that fate? What is the meaning of that "depart" which is Jesus's sentence upon those who work iniquity? About this question also there can be no doubt. The Sermon on the Mount itself gives the answer: "If your right eye causes you to sin, tear it out and throw it away. For it is better that you lose one of your members than that your whole body be thrown into hell" (Matt 5:29). The answer is given also in the whole teaching of Jesus, and it is implied even in the verses with which we now have to do. No, there can be no doubt whatever about what Jesus meant by that word "depart"; he meant that those upon whom he would pronounce that sentence to depart would be cast into hell.

The thought of hell as well as the thought of heaven runs all through the teaching of Jesus; it gives to his ethical teaching that stupendous earnestness which is its marked characteristic. But how is hell here designated? It is described elsewhere in the Gospels; and never let us forget, whether we call the language "figurative" or not, that it means an eternal and terrible punishment, a punishment of which there is no end. But how is hell designated in this particular passage? The answer may be surprising to some people, but it is perfectly plain. Hell is designed in our passage as being banishment from Jesus.

I do just beg you to think of that for a moment, my friends. Jesus of Nazareth certainly did believe—no good historian can deny it—that he would sit upon the judgment-seat of God at the terrible last judgment day, that his word would be final, and that life in his presence would be heaven and departure from him would be hell.

What has become of the weak, sentimental, purely human, purely ethical Jesus of modern reconstruction; what has become of your Jesus who was a simple teacher of righteousness and advanced no claim to be God? Have you found your purely human Jesus, and have you escaped from the divine Christ of the creeds, by appealing from the Gospel according to John to the Sermon on the Mount? No, indeed, my friend. The Jesus of the Bible is everywhere exactly the same.

What will you do with Jesus? Will you treat him with a mild approval? Ah, people are so patronizing in the presence of Jesus today. They say such kind, polite things about him. They are good enough to say that his ethics will solve the problems of society; they are good enough to say that he enunciated some maxims that are better than Jefferson's ten rules and go far beyond Socrates and Confucius and Buddha. They are perfectly ready to let him influence some departments of their life. They will not receive him as their Savior; they are not interested in his atoning blood, but they are so complacent in his presence.

God grant that it may not be so with you, my friends! God grant that you may never treat Jesus with this polite, patronizing approval! God grant that you may not treat him as a religious genius or as the founder of one of the world's religions! God grant that, instead, you may say to Jesus, with doubting Thomas: "My Lord and my God" (John 20:28).

FIVE

What Jesus Said about Himself

We have discussed the deity of Christ as it is attested by Jesus himself in the Sermon on the Mount. We have seen that in the very passage to which unbelievers appeal in support of their view that Jesus kept himself out of his gospel and merely presented a program of life to be followed first by him and then by his followers—in that very passage Jesus presents himself as possessed of an authority that goes far beyond that of any prophet and is in truth an authority that belongs only to God. At the close of our last talk, we were speaking particularly of the passage near the end of the Sermon on the Mount where Jesus presents himself as the one who is to sit at the last day on the judgment-seat of God and determine the eternal destinies of all the world.

This is by no means the only passage in the Gospels where

Jesus so presents himself as the final judge. Indeed, it is probably because of this thought of himself as the final judge that he uses one of his favorite titles to designate himself—namely, the title "the Son of man."

Our first impulse might be to say that the title is a designation of the humanity of Jesus as distinguished from his deity. He was both God and man, and that, we may be tempted to say, is what he meant when he called himself "Son of man" as well as "Son of God.'

If that view of the title were correct, it would certainly be a very lofty title, and it would certainly not be in any contradiction with the deity of Christ. But, as a matter of fact, it is unlikely that the title "the Son of man" on the lips of Jesus has this meaning at all. It is unlikely that it is intended to designate the humanity of our Lord as distinguished from his deity. It is on the whole unlikely that there is any contrast in the Gospels between the title "Son of man" and the title "Son of God." People who use these titles to designate the two natures of Jesus as both man and God, who call attention, in other words, to the fact that he was both "Son of man" and "Son of God," are probably wrong in their interpretation of the title, right though they unquestionably are in holding that Jesus was both God and man.

The true key to the title "Son of man" on the lips of our Lord is probably to be found in the seventh chapter of the book of Daniel, where "one like a son of man" (Dan 7:13) appears in the presence of the "Ancient of Days" and receives an everlasting dominion. When this person is said to be "one like a son of man," that is not said because he is a man in contrast with God. The contrast is rather with the beasts—lion, bear, leopard, and unnamed beast—that represent the world empires preceding the kingdom of the one like unto a son of man. After the successive appearance of those kingdoms represented by figures designated as being each like the figure of some beast, there arises a kingdom whose ruler appears in the vision as a man. That kingdom unlike those other kingdoms is to be everlasting.

This passage in the book of Daniel had an important influence upon subsequent Messianic expectations among the Jews. In the so-called Ethiopic book of Enoch, for example—a book which of course is not in the Bible and does not at all deserve to be there—the title "the Son of man" occurs frequently as the designation of a heavenly personage already existing in heaven but destined to appear in great glory to be the judge of all the world. Now we certainly do not mean for one moment that our Lord made any use of that so-called book of Enoch. But the thing that *is* likely is that that book does give evidence of the use among the Jews of the great passage in the seventh chapter of Daniel. On the basis of that passage the coming Deliverer had come to be called—in certain Jewish circles at least—"the Son of man," and had come to be thought of as destined to appear with the clouds of heaven and be the judge of all the earth. What our Lord did when he called himself "the Son of man" was to place the stamp of approval upon this Jewish expectation because it was really in accordance with the Old Testament, and then to apply it to himself.

It is altogether probable, then, that the title "the Son of man" on the lips of Jesus is distinctly a Messianic title. It does not designate the humanity of Jesus as distinguished from his deity, but it designates him as being that transcendent, heavenly person who was to come one day with the clouds of heaven and be the final judge of all the world.

A notable passage in the book of Acts confirms this view of the title "the Son of man." In Acts 7:55–56, it is said, of the dying martyr Stephen:

> But he, full of the Holy Spirit, gazed into heaven and saw the glory of God, and Jesus standing at the right hand of God. And he said, "Behold, I see the heavens opened, and the Son of Man standing at the right hand of God."

Here the reference to the seventh chapter of Daniel is perfectly plain. Stephen sees essentially the same vision as that which the prophet Daniel had seen; he sees that heavenly figure, the Son of man, appearing in glory in the presence of God.

As Jesus uses the title, the origin of the title is just as clear as it is in the words of the dying Stephen. So, for example, in Mark 8:38 (with the parallel passages):

> For whoever is ashamed of me and of my words in this adulterous and sinful generation, of him will the Son of Man also be ashamed when he comes in the glory of his Father with the holy angels.

So also in Mark 13:26 (with the parallel passages):

> And then they will see the Son of Man coming in clouds with great power and glory.

In such passages the reference to the great scene in the seventh chapter of Daniel is perfectly clear.

In other passages, it is true, the reference to that scene is not so direct. Jesus sometimes uses the title the Son of man where he is speaking not of his exaltation but of his humiliation. So in Matthew 8:20, where it is said that the "the Son of Man has nowhere to lay his head." So also in the great passage Mark 10:45, where Jesus says, regarding his atoning death, that "the Son of

Man came not to be served but to serve, and to give his life as a ransom for many." But we may fairly hold that the use of the title in these passages is intended to *contrast* the stupendous dignity properly belonging to the Son of man, the judge and ruler of all the world, with his present humble life. The real pathos of those passages is found in the fact that it was not any ordinary man who had nowhere to lay his head, and that it was not any ordinary man who came not to be ministered unto but to minister, but the heavenly Son of man, that stupendous figure, who was now more homeless than the foxes and the birds!

Here and there, as Jesus uses the title, there may possibly be a special reference to the humanity of the one so designated, but such passages at the most are rare, and the prevailing significance of the title is that it identifies Jesus with the heavenly Messiah, the stupendous figure spoken of in the seventh chapter of Daniel whose kingdom would be an everlasting kingdom.

That, I may say in passing, is the prevailing opinion today among scholars of widely different shades of opinion, both believers and unbelievers. Here and there a defender of another view of the title appears, but I think it may be said that the prevailing view among careful scholars is what I have just indicated. For a full discussion of this subject, I want to refer you to a book to which I have been much indebted—the learned book of Dr. Geerhardus Vos on *The Self-Disclosure of Jesus*.

What particularly needs to be said, however, is that whatever view be taken of the origin and meaning of the term "the Son of man," it is at any rate clear that Jesus of Nazareth certainly did claim that he would one day sit on the judgment-seat of God to decide the eternal destinies of men. That claim appears, as we observed very clearly, in the Sermon on the Mount. You cannot get away from it even in the supposedly purely ethical parts of Jesus's teaching. It runs all through the Gospels. Every historian, whether he is a Christian or not, ought to take account of this strange fact—that a certain Jesus, a man who lived in the first century in Palestine, was actually convinced, as he looked out upon the men who thronged about him, that he would one day sit on the judgment-seat of God and be their judge and the judge and ruler of all the world.

What are you going to do with that claim of Jesus? If you hold it to be true, then Jesus is your King and Lord. If you hold it to be false, then I do not see how in the world you can go on taking him as a worthy example for your life.

The conviction of Jesus that he would at the last judgment decide the eternal destinies of men was joined with the conviction that he could determine those eternal destinies here and now. He claimed to be able to forgive sins. His opponents got the point of that claim; they got it far better than certain modern persons who trip along so lightly over the things that the Gospels contain. "Why does this man speak like that?" they said. "He is blaspheming! Who can forgive sins but God alone?" (Mark 2:7). They were right. None can forgive sins but God only. Jesus was a blasphemer if he was a mere man. At that point the enemies saw clearly. You may accept the lofty claims of Jesus. You may take him as very God. Or else you must reject him as a miserable, deluded enthusiast. There is really no middle ground. Jesus refuses to be pressed into the mold of a mere religious teacher.

Thus we have seen that Jesus's claim of deity runs all through the Gospels. It does not appear merely in this passage or that, but is really presupposed in every word that Jesus uttered and in everything that he did.

There was, it is true, a period in his ministry when he did not make his own person for the most part the express subject of his teaching. It was always the background of his teaching and his work; without it everything that he said and did becomes unintelligible. But during a large part of his Galilean ministry, as described by the Synoptic Gospels, he seems not often to have set forth the mystery of his own person in any detailed way.

That lack is wonderfully supplied by the Gospel according to John, which was written by a man who stood in the innermost circle of the disciples of our Lord. But what I want you to observe particularly is that there is no opposition at this point between the Fourth Gospel and the other three. The Christ who is so gloriously set forth in the Gospel according to John is exactly the Christ who is everywhere presupposed in the Synoptic Gospels. Far from being in any contradiction with the Synoptic Gospels, the Gospel according to John, with its rich report of the teaching of our Lord about his own person, provides the key which enables us the better to understand what we are told in Matthew, Mark, and Luke.

Here and there, moreover, we have in the Synoptic Gospels just the kind of teaching of our Lord about himself as that which appears so fully reported by the beloved disciple in the Gospel according to John. That is notably the case with a famous passage in the eleventh chapter of Matthew, which has a close parallel in the tenth chapter of Luke. "All things have been handed over to me by my Father," says Jesus, "and no one knows the Son except the Father, and no one knows the Father except the Son and anyone to whom the Son chooses to reveal him" (Matt 11:27; Luke 10:22). Here we have not only the substance of the teaching that appears so fully in the fourth Gospel but even the form of it, "*the* Father," "*the* Son"—how often those terms appear set over against each other in the Gospel according to John just exactly as they are set over against each other here!

Just consider how wonderfully rich is the content of this verse in its report of the teaching of Jesus about himself! "No one knows the Father except the Son"—that in itself is a very stupendous utterance. It designates Jesus as truly knowing God, and as the only one who knows him. We think instinctively, as we read, of the words in the Gospel according to John: "No one has ever seen God; the only God, who is at the Father's side, he has made him known" (John 1:18). How wonderful is such a knowledge of God! Think of it, my friends. Jesus of Nazareth, a man walking upon this earth, said as he talked to his contemporaries: "No one knows the Father save me." How is such rich knowledge of God possible to any but God himself?

But that is not all that there is in this saying. No, the saying goes far beyond that. "No one knows the Father except the Son"—that is wonderful enough. But that is not all. There is something still more stupendous in this verse. It is this: "No one knows the Son except the Father."

Just think what these words mean, my friends. They mean that there are mysteries in the person, Jesus, which none but the infinite and eternal God can know. The two persons, the Father and the Son, are here put in a strange reciprocal relationship. They are both mysterious to all others, but they are known, and fully known, to each other. The Son knows the depths of the Father's being, and the Father knows the depths of the being of the Son. An ineffable mutual knowledge prevails between these two.

What does that mean? It means what is really implied in

the Gospels from beginning to end. It means that that strange man who is known to history as Jesus of Nazareth was no mere man, but the infinite and eternal and unchangeable God. In this wonderful verse, the twenty-seventh verse of the eleventh chapter of Matthew, we have in summary and in implication the great doctrine of the deity of our Lord, and when we put it together with Jesus's teaching regarding the Holy Spirit we have the full wonderful teaching of Scripture regarding the three persons in one God.

I have not time in the present talk to speak to you longer about that doctrine; I have not time to set forth further the richness of the Scripture's testimony to the deity of our blessed Lord. But there is one thing that I do want to drive home at once.

It is this: this mysterious verse of which we have just been speaking does not appear as some excrescence in the Gospel picture of Jesus but as an integral part of the whole. When we come upon this "christological" passage in our reading of the Gospel of Matthew, this passage which has been called "the Johannine passage" because it is so much like the Gospel according to John, do we feel anything like a shock? Do we feel as though we were transplanted into another atmosphere? Do we feel as though we were suddenly dealing with another Christ?

I tell you, my friends, we do not. No, we are dealing with the same Christ as the Christ with whom we have been dealing all through the Gospel according to Matthew; we are dealing with exactly the same Christ as the Christ who spoke, for example, the Sermon on the Mount. We are dealing with the same Christ as the Christ who, according to all four Gospels, spoke words of solemn warning but also words of an infinite tenderness and grace.

What is the context of this verse with which we have been dealing in the present talk—this verse which sets forth in such stupendous fashion the majesty of the person of our Lord? Just let me read it to you before we part:

> I thank you, Father, Lord of heaven and earth, that you
> have hidden these things from the wise and understand-
> ing and revealed them to little children; yes, Father, for
> such was your gracious will. (Matt 11:25–26)

Then follow the words of which we have spoken, the words in which Jesus speaks of that ineffable relation between the Father and the Son. Then what follows? Does something follow that reveals some later theology of the church, something that fails to show the unmistakable, characteristic, inimitable quality of Jesus's authentic teaching? Judge for yourselves, my friends. Here is what follows upon that stupendous testimony to the deity of Christ:

Come to me, all who labor and are heavy laden, and I will give you rest. Take my yoke upon you, and learn from me, for I am gentle and lowly in heart, and you will find rest for your souls. For my yoke is easy, and my burden is light. (Matt 11:28–30)

Are those the words of some falsifier who put upon the lips of Jesus words that Jesus never spoke? Are those the words of some religious genius who used the name of Jesus as the medium through which he might convey his teaching to the world?

Oh, no, my friends; no religious genius ever spoke words like these. These are words such as never man spake.

How sweet these words are on the lips of Jesus! How abominable they would be on the lips of any other! "Come to me, all who labor and are heavy laden, and I will give you rest"—who could speak those words without mocking and deceiving those who hear? I will tell you. Only he who said in the same breath: "No one knows the Son except the Father, and no one knows the Father except the Son." The plain fact is that that gracious invitation of Jesus—an invitation so sweetly repeated again and again in the Gospels by him who was sent to seek and to save that which was lost—the plain fact is that that invitation is a divine invitation. The one who uttered it was a deceiver or he was God.

Yet, it is objected, there are so many who will not accept the invitation; there are so many learned men who will not believe Jesus when he advances these stupendous claims. Yes, I know. They are very many and they are very learned.

But did not Jesus himself say so; did not Jesus himself say that there were many learned persons who would ever learnedly reject him when he offered himself as their Savior and Lord? "I thank you, Father, Lord of heaven and earth, that you have hidden these things from the wise and understanding and revealed them to little children."

Which are you, my friends? Do you belong to the wise and prudent, of whom our Lord spoke? Do you belong to those who rely upon the wisdom of this world and turn aside from Christ? Or are you among the babes? Will you come to Jesus weak and helpless; will you come to him as a very little child? Are you weary and heavy laden? Will you come to him that he may give you rest?

SIX

The Supernatural Christ

I have been talking to you about the deity of Christ, and have shown you that Jesus's testimony to his own deity is not found merely in the Gospel according to John. It is found in all four Gospels and it pervades all parts of the Gospels. Even in the so-called ethical parts of the Gospels like the Sermon on the Mount the stupendous claim of Jesus is really presupposed.

We must now, however, notice something else. We must notice that this claim of Jesus is everywhere supported by his power to work miracles. That is the way in which the Gospels represent the miracles. They represent them as attestations to show that Jesus spoke the truth when he came forward with his stupendous claim.

This biblical estimate of the miracles has often been reversed in the minds of modern men. The miracles, men tell us, even if they really happened, are at best an obstacle to faith rather than an aid to faith. People used to believe, they tell us, because of the miracles; they now believe, if they believe at all, in spite of the miracles.

A curious confusion underlies this way of thinking. In one sense, of course it is true that the miracles are an obstacle to faith. Unquestionably, a narrative that has no miracles in it is easier to believe than a narrative that contains miracles. Of course that is so. Who ever denied it? A perfectly trivial narrative is easier to believe than one that contains an account of extraordinary happenings. So, if I should tell you that when I walked down the street today I saw a Ford car, my narrative would have at least one advantage over the narratives in the New Testament—it would certainly be far easier to believe. But then it would also have one disadvantage. It would be far easier to believe, but then, you see, it would not be worth believing.

So, if the Gospels contained no miracles they would in one sense be easier to believe than they are now. But, do you not see the thing that would be believed would be entirely different from the thing that is believed now when we take the Gospels as they stand? If the Jesus of the Gospels were a purely natural and not a supernatural person, then we should have no difficulty in believing that such a person lived in the first century of our era. Even skeptics would have no difficulty in believing it. Defenders of the faith would have an easy victory indeed. Everybody would believe. But then there would be one drawback. It would be this: the thing that everybody would believe would not be worth believing.

A purely natural, as distinguished from a supernatural, Christ would be just a teacher and example. There have been many teachers and examples in the history of mankind. It would place no particular demands upon our faith if we were told that this teacher and example was a little better than any of the others. But then, you see, we are not looking for a teacher and example. We are looking for a Savior. And a purely human, a merely natural, as distinguished from a supernatural, Christ can never be our Savior. He would merely be one of us. He would need a Savior for himself before he could save others; he just as much as we would need a supernatural Savior.

We have such a Savior presented to us in the Gospels, a Savior who is not merely man but God. The really difficult thing to believe is that such a Savior really entered into this world. It is a very blessed thing, but it is certainly not a trivial thing. It is not one of those trivial things that are so easy to believe because they occur every day. It is certainly not a thing that can be believed without a mighty revolution in all a man's thinking and all a man's life.

If now you ask whether it would be easier to believe *that thing* without the individual miracles narrated in the Gospels than it is to believe it with those individual miracles, we answer emphatically, "No." It would be easier to believe the story of a mere religious teacher without the miracles. Certainly. That goes without saying. But not to believe the story of the life upon earth of the incarnate Son of God. The whole appearance of such a divine person upon earth is itself a stupendous miracle. The individual miracles, with their individual attestation, do make it easier to believe that great central miracle. They are proofs of it. They are exactly what the Bible represents them as being—true testimonies to the truth of that stupendous claim of Jesus to be very God.

If you examine carefully the views of those who reject the individual miracles, you will discover that they do not really hold on to the great central and all-pervading miracle. They may seem to do so. They use the old terminology. They love to speak of "incarnation"; they love to speak of God as having become man. But when you come to look at them closely, you discover that this use of traditional terminology on their part only serves to mask from them themselves and from others a profound difference of thought. They mean by "incarnation" just about the opposite of what the Bible means by it. They do not really mean by it that the eternal Son of God, the second person of the Trinity, became man this once, and this once only, "and so was, and continueth to be God, and man, in two distinct natures, and one person, forever" (WSC Q&A 21). No, they mean something entirely different. They are very far indeed from believing on Christ for salvation as he is offered to us in the gospel.

The truth is that the Bible's picture of Jesus possesses a wonderful unity. Without the miracles as the Gospels narrate them the unity would be sadly destroyed. Every one of the miracles, with its historical attestation, adds its quota of evidence to our great central conviction that this Jesus is indeed the Son of God.

It is interesting to observe the way in which the miracles of the life of Christ have been treated in the history of modern unbelief. The cardinal principle of unbelief is that miracles have never happened. What, then, shall be done with the accounts of miracles that are found in the Gospels?

The first impulse of a skeptic might be to say that since the Gospel picture of Jesus contains miracles, and since miracles never happened, therefore the whole picture is untrue. But that of course will not do at all. It is perfectly clear that we have in the Gospels an account of a real person who really lived in Palestine in the first century of our era. The picture is entirely too lifelike ever to have been the product of invention. That is admitted by all except a few extremists. Very well, then. If the picture is the picture of a real person, what shall be done with the miracles that it contains? Those miracles, according to the initial assumption of our skeptical investigator, never happened; yet they are narrated in an account of a real historical person. What shall be done about it?

The obvious answer of unbelievers is that the miracles must be rejected in order to leave the rest. In this way, it is supposed, we shall be able to sift the material in the Gospels in order to arrive at the modicum of truth that they contain. When, it is said, we have removed from the Gospel picture of Jesus these gaudy colors of the supernatural we shall have Jesus as he actually was.

Well, it sounds easy. Surely it must have been accomplished long before now—the removal of the miracles from the picture of Jesus in the Gospels. Many of the most brilliant of modern men have been engaged in it during the past hundred years. Surely their efforts must have been successful.

That is certainly what one might expect. But in this case expectations are not borne out by the fact. The plain fact is that this "quest of the historical Jesus," as it has been called—this effort to take the miracles out of the Gospels—has proved to be a colossal failure. It is being increasingly recognized as being a failure even by the skeptical historians themselves. The supernatural is found to be far more deeply rooted in the Gospel account of Jesus than was formerly supposed.

At first, it seemed to be quite easy to get the miracles out of the Gospels. All we shall have to do, said the skeptical historians, is just to take the miracles out and leave all the rest. Even the miracle-incidents themselves, they said, can be accepted as historical; only, we must observe that they were not really miraculous. So Luke tells us in the first chapter that Zacharias the father of John the Baptist went into the temple at the hour of incense and received an announcement about the birth of a son. Is that incident historical? Did Zacharias really go into the temple that day? Certainly, said the men of this way of thinking, the incident is historical; certainly Zacharias went into the temple. Of course he was slightly mistaken about what he saw! He thought he saw an angel when what he really saw was just the smoke rising from the altar in that dim religious light. But such mistakes do not cast any general discredit upon the narratives in which they stand.

So also all four of the Gospels say that Jesus one day fed five thousand men. Is that incident historical? Did Jesus really feed those five thousand men? Certainly the narrative is historical, said the men of the way of thinking with which we are now dealing; certainly Jesus fed those five thousand men. What he did was just to take those five loaves and two fishes and set a good example by distributing them to the people immediately around him. That led the other fortunate people among the crowd to do likewise. His good example was contagious. People who were fortunate enough to have any food distributed it to those around them and so everybody was fed. Thus the incident is perfectly historical but it was not really miraculous. The whole trouble has come from the fact that readers of the Gospels have insisted on putting a supernaturalistic interpretation upon an incident that was really quite natural.

It is all perfectly easy and simple, is it not? How nicely the task has been accomplished—miracles as neatly extracted as an appendix is extracted in a modern hospital, everything else allowed to remain "as was," the general trustworthiness of the Gospels rescued, Jesus made to keep within the bounds of nature's laws! What was all the bother about? It was all so perfectly simple!

Such was the so-called "rationalizing" method of dealing with the miracle narratives, as practiced by Paulus and others one hundred years ago. It had considerable vogue in its day. But its vogue was of short duration. God raised up a besom of destruction for it in the person of a disconcerting young man named David Friedrich Strauss.

Strauss published his *Life of Jesus* in 1835. It was unquestionably one of the most influential books of modern times—a very important book to have been written by a young man of twenty-seven years of age.

I said that Strauss's book was influential. I did not say that its influence was good, and as a matter of fact, it was not good but very bad. Strauss did not write in the interests of the truth of the Gospels; he did not write from the point of view of a real

Christian believer. On the contrary, he wrote from the point of view of extreme unbelief. His book remains to the present day perhaps the fullest compendium of what can be said against the truthfulness of the Gospel narratives.

Yet such a book had at least the use, in the providence of God, of demolishing the rationalizing method of dealing with the miracle-narratives in the Gospels. In those narratives, Strauss said, the miracles are the main thing; they are the thing for which all the rest exists. How absurd, then, to say that the narratives have grown up out of utterly trivial events upon which a supernaturalistic interpretation was wrongly put! No, said Strauss, we must give up all attempts at finding a modicum of historical truth in these narratives; they are simply myths—that is, they are popular expressions, in narrative form, of certain religious ideas; they are merely the way in which popular fancy expressed the great debt which the early Christian church owed to Jesus.

At first, Strauss's book caused great consternation. He had not, indeed, denied the historical existence of Jesus, and of course he really held that much that is narrated about Jesus in the Gospels is true. But so radical was his criticism, and so completely did he fail to put together into any continuous positive account of Jesus what was left after his criticism had done its work, that it was quite natural for people to feel that Strauss had almost removed Jesus of Nazareth from the pages of history.

Then, however, an attempt was made to repair the damage. I am not referring to the defense of the Gospels by believing scholars, but I am referring to the attempt by men of Strauss's own way of thinking—men, that is, who like Strauss denied the occurrence of miracles—to discover and make use of the modicum of truth that might be thought to remain in the Gospels after criticism had been given its rights.

Possibly, it was supposed, that modicum of truth might be discovered by what is called "source-criticism." The Gospels, it was admitted, contain much that is untrue, but if we could discover the earlier sources used by the writers of the Gospels we might get much nearer to the facts. Well, an imposing attempt was made in that direction. The Gospel according to John was rejected as almost altogether unhistorical, and then the two chief sources of Matthew and Luke were held to be (1) Mark and (2) a lost source composed chiefly of sayings of Jesus as distinguished from accounts of his deeds. That was the famous "two-document theory" for the sources of the Gospels.

On the basis of that theory a supposedly historical account of a purely human Jesus was constructed. People became quite enthusiastic about it. The troublesome miracles, it was supposed, were all removed; the theological Christ of the creeds was done away. But, it was said, something better had been rediscovered—a really and purely human Jesus, a Jesus who was one of us, a Jesus who started where we started and won through to sonship with God, a Jesus who kept his own person out of his gospel and simply taught—by word and by life—the great liberating truths of the fatherhood of God and the brotherhood of man.

Such was the so-called "Liberal Jesus." It was an imposing reconstruction indeed. It was thought to offer great promise to the human race. The shackles of dogma, it was supposed, had been removed. A new Reformation would soon take place.

But alas for human hopes! Nothing has been seen of the new reformation, and the imposing reconstruction of the Liberal Jesus has fallen to the ground. I think the first thirty-five years of the twentieth century might almost be called, in the sphere of New Testament criticism, the period of the decline and fall of "the Liberal Jesus." That is a great outstanding fact. I think that it is a fact that is going to loom up very large to future historians when the history of the period in which we are living comes finally to be written.

The great trouble is that the miraculous in the Gospels is found to be much more pervasive than it was at first thought to be. It runs through the Gospels as we now have them. That is clear. But it also is found to run through the sources supposed rightly or wrongly to underlie the Gospels. All right, then; suppose we go even back of those earliest written sources and examine supposed detached bits of oral tradition out of which they are sometimes supposed to have been composed. Alas, we obtain no relief. Those supposed detached bits are found themselves to contain the objectionable miraculous element. There seems to be no escape from the supernatural Christ. At the very beginning of the church—not at some later time but at the very beginning—Jesus was regarded not just as a religious teacher or just as a prophet but as a supernatural Deliverer.

That is the result at which ultra-modern criticism has arrived. It is a far cry from the cheerful, rationalizing days of Paulus one hundred years ago. It is a far cry from the time when men thought they could explain away this miracle-narrative and that, and have a perfectly good account left of a great religious teacher.

The outstanding result of a hundred years of effort to separate the natural from the supernatural in the early Christian view of Jesus is that the thing cannot be done. The two are inseparable. The very earliest early Christian account of Jesus is found to be supernaturalistic to the core.

Very well, what shall we do about it? The earliest view of Jesus that we know anything about represents him as a supernatural person. It is found to exhibit a remarkable unanimity at this point. What shall we do with it? There are only two things to do with it. We can take it or we can leave it.

Modern skeptical historians are saying we must leave it. All our information about Jesus is supernaturalistic, they are saying; therefore, all our information about Jesus is uncertain. We can never disentangle the real Jesus from the beliefs of his earliest followers. The only Christ we really know is the supernatural Christ of Jesus's earliest followers. We can never rediscover the portrait of the real Jesus.

Are you afraid of skepticism like that? I am not afraid of it a bit. It is easily refuted by a mere reading of the Gospels. I beg you just to read the Gospels for yourselves, my friends, and then ask yourselves whether the person here presented to you is not a living, breathing person. The extreme skepticism of the day will always be refuted by common sense.

That being so, the extreme skepticism of our day is very instructive. I get great comfort from it. Do you not see, my friends? That extreme skepticism of Bultmann and others is the inevitable result of trying to reject the miracles in the Gospels. That extreme skepticism is absurd. What is the conclusion? The conclusion is that the process which inevitably led to that extreme skepticism was wrong from the beginning. We never ought to have tried to reject the miracles in the Gospels at all.

I wonder when men are going to draw this conclusion. It does seem to lie so very near at hand. When will they cease to be blind to it? The Gospels present to us just one Christ—the supernatural Christ. They do so with overwhelmingly self-evidencing force. When shall we just accept their witness? When shall we just say that God did walk upon this earth? When shall we just come to that divine Christ and ask him to be the Savior of our souls?

SEVEN

Did Christ Rise from the Dead?

I n the last of these talks, I was speaking to you about the miracles of Christ. But a treatment of the miracles would be incom-
plete unless we singled out for special examination the central or
crowning miracle, which is the miracle of the resurrection.

In treating the resurrection, I suggest that we may begin with
things about which everybody is agreed, in order that we may go
on from them to speak of things with regard to which Christian
people differ from those who are not Christians.

Nineteen hundred years ago there lived in an obscure corner
of the Roman Empire one who would have seemed to a super-
ficial observer to be a remarkable man. He engaged in a career
of religious teaching accompanied by a ministry of healing. At
first he had the favor of the crowd, but since he would not be

the kind of leader the people demanded he soon fell victim to the jealousy of the rulers of his people and to the cowardice of the Roman governor. He died the death of criminals of that day, on the cross.

At his death, his followers were discouraged. They had evidently been far inferior to him in discernment and in courage, and now what little courage they may have had was gone. His death meant the destruction of all their hopes. Never, one might have said, was a movement more completely dead than the movement which had been begun by Jesus of Nazareth.

Then, however, the surprising thing happened. It is a fact of history, which no real historian denies, that those same weak, discouraged men, the followers of Jesus, began, within a very short time after the shameful death of their leader, in Jerusalem, the scene of their cowardly flight, the most remarkable religious movement that the world has ever known, the movement commonly called the Christian church.

At first, that movement was obscure. But it spread like wildfire. In a few decades at the most it was firmly planted in the chief cities of the civilized world and in Rome itself. After a lapse of less than three centuries it conquered the Roman Empire. Incalculable has been its influence upon the whole history of the world.

What caused that remarkable change in those followers of

Jesus? What caused those weak and cowardly men suddenly to become the spiritual conquerors of the world? At that point the difference of opinion arises. Yet even with regard to that point there is a certain measure of agreement. It is now admitted by historians both Christian and non-Christian that those followers of Jesus became the founders of what is commonly known as the Christian church because they became honestly convinced that Jesus was risen from the dead.

But what in turn produced that conviction? What produced the belief of the first disciples in the resurrection of Christ? There is where the difference of opinion comes in.

The New Testament, of course, has a perfectly clear answer to the question. The belief of the disciples in the resurrection, according to the New Testament, was due simply to the fact of the resurrection. Those disciples came to believe that Jesus had risen from the dead for the simple reason that Jesus *had* risen from the dead. He had risen from the dead; and they had not only seen his tomb empty but had seen him alive after his death on the cross.

If that explanation of the belief of the first disciples in the resurrection be rejected, what shall be put into its place? The answer to that question which is given today by all or practically all unbelievers is that those first disciples of Jesus became convinced that Jesus had risen from the dead because they experienced certain hallucinations, certain pathological experiences in which they thought they saw Jesus before their eyes when in reality there was nothing there. In an hallucination, the optic nerve is really affected but it is affected not by light rays coming from an external object, but by some pathological condition of the bodily organism of the subject himself. This is the so-called "vision theory" regarding the origin of the Christian church. It has held the field among unbelievers inside of the church and outside of the church since the days of Strauss about one hundred years ago.

I think we ought to understand just exactly what that vision theory means. It means that the Christian church is founded upon a pathological experience of certain persons in the first century of our era. It means that if there had been a good neurologist for Peter and the others to consult there never would have been a Christian church.

I am perfectly well aware of the fact that advocates of the vision hypothesis refuse to look at the matter just exactly in that way. The really important thing, they say, was not the pathological experience which those men had, but it was the impression left upon them by Jesus's character. They never would have experienced those hallucinations, they say, unless their minds and hearts had been filled with the thought of the radiant personality of Jesus. It was because they were so much impressed with him that they came to have those hallucinations. Thus the hallucinations, say the advocates of the vision hypothesis, were merely the temporary form which was necessary in that day and among men of that kind of education in order that the influence of Jesus could continue to make itself felt. *We*, they say, can get rid of that form. We no longer need to believe that Jesus rose from the dead and appeared to the eyes of his disciples. But we can still let the influence of Jesus be felt in our lives. In the changed lives of men who have been influenced by him, Jesus has his truest resurrection.

So the thing is represented by the advocates of what is mis-leadingly called a "spiritual resurrection." This representation altogether ignores the real character of the first disciples' faith. What those men had from the appearances of the risen Christ was not merely the conviction that Jesus was still alive. No, what they had was the conviction that he had risen. It was not merely the *state* of Jesus resultant upon the resurrection which was valu-able for them, but the act of the resurrection. At the heart of their faith was the conviction that Jesus had *done* something for them by his death and resurrection. The Christian religion in other words is rooted in an event.

If that supposed event really took place, as the Bible says it did, then the Christian religion is true. If it did not take place, as the dominant vision theory holds, then the Christian religion is false, and a church that professes it is merely an empty shell.

But is the message upon which the Christian church is founded really true? Did Christ rise from the dead?

I want to say just a few words to you about that subject now. Two things are to be noted about the account of the appearances which the New Testament contains.

The first thing concerns the manner of the appearances. The appearances, according to the New Testament, were of a plain bodily kind. Jesus did not, it is true, simply resume the conditions of his life before the crucifixion. There was something mysterious about his coming and going. Yet he is plainly represented as being with his disciples in body. They could touch him. He partook of food in their presence. He held extended conversations with them.

The second feature of the appearances, as they are described in the New Testament, concerns the place of the appearances. The appearances, according to the New Testament, were both at Jerusalem and in Galilee; and the first appearances were at Jerusalem.

Both these features of the New Testament account of the appearances are rejected by advocates of the vision hypothesis. The former feature is always rejected by them, the latter usually.

The advocates of the vision hypothesis hold, with regard to the manner of the appearances, that, contrary to the New Testament, the appearances were only of a momentary kind. The disciples who experienced the appearances did not experience any extended intercourse with Jesus. They not only did not *really* have any extended intercourse with him, but they did not even *think* they had any extended intercourse with him. All they even thought they had was a momentary sight of him in glory or perhaps the sound of a word or two of his ringing in their ears. The New Testament is quite wrong in saying they even thought they saw or heard any more than that.

The second point at which the advocates of the vision hypothesis, or most of them, reject the New Testament account of the appearances concerns the place of the appearances. Most of the advocates of the vision hypothesis hold that the first of the "appearances"—which they of course regard as hallucinations—took place a considerable time, perhaps weeks, after the crucifixion, in Galilee; the New Testament says that the first of the appearances took place at Jerusalem on the third day after the death of Jesus.

At first sight it might look as though this were a mere difference in detail. But that is not so. As a matter of fact, it is a difference of a very important kind.

If the first appearances, the first of these supposed hallucinations in which the disciples thought they saw Jesus alive after his death, took pace at Jerusalem and on the third day after the death, then the question arises why the tomb of Jesus was not investigated to see whether the story of the resurrection was really true—why it was not investigated by foes as well as by friends. If the resurrection was not a fact, then the investigation of the tomb of Jesus would refute the story, and the beginning of the Christian church would have been prevented.

If, on the other hand, the first appearances took place in Galilee weeks after the death of Jesus, then, it might be said, when the disciples finally did return to Jerusalem it would be too late for the tomb to be investigated. Thus the so-called Galilean hypothesis as to the place of the first appearances might be thought to remove the difficulty which a consideration of the tomb of Jesus has always placed in the way of a denial of the fact of the resurrection.

What shall be said about that? Two things are to be said about it.

In the first place, even the Galilean hypothesis does not really remove the difficulty, since it does seem strange even on the Galilean hypothesis that the tomb of Jesus was not investigated, and, in the second place, the Galilean hypothesis is not true.

Where shall we turn to test the hypothesis of unbelievers, not only on this point regarding the place of the appearances but also on the point regarding the manner of the appearances?

Well, we can of course turn to the Gospels. We can show that the low view which unbelievers hold regarding the Gospels is not justified and that these documents are really trustworthy accounts of what the first disciples of Jesus said with regard to the founding of the church.

But obviously it would be a good thing also if we could find some source of information which is admitted to be good not only by believers but also by unbelievers. Can we find such a source of information? Can we find a source of information with regard to which there is some common meeting ground between ourselves and our opponents in this debate?

The answer is, "Yes." We can find such a source of information in the First Epistle to the Corinthians. It is generally admitted by foes of our view as well as by friends that that epistle was really written by the apostle Paul and that it was written at about AD 55, approximately twenty-five years after the death of Jesus. It is also generally admitted that when Paul says in this epistle that he had "received" the information that he gives in the fifteenth chapter regarding the resurrection and appearances of Jesus he means that he had received it from the early Jerusalem church—particularly, perhaps, from Peter, with whom he tells us in another of his epistles that he spent fifteen days only three years after his conversion. What we have here, then, in the fifteenth chapter of this epistle, in verse eight and the following verses, is a precious bit of what modern historians call "primitive tradition." It is usually admitted by friends and foes of our view that we have here a summary of what the very earliest Jerusalem church said about the events that lay at the beginning of its life.

Well, then, is this account by the primitive Jerusalem church of the resurrection and related events favorable to the contention of unbelievers—the contention that at the beginning the appearances were regarded as independent of what had become of the body of Jesus? Volumes have been written about this question. But the answer, if we may put it plainly and briefly, is most emphatically, "No." This passage is not favorable to the contention of unbelievers at all.

What does Paul say exactly when he summarizes that precious tradition of the earliest Jerusalem church? Here is what he says:

> For I delivered to you as of first importance what I also received: that Christ died for our sins in accordance with the Scriptures, that he was buried, that he was raised on the third day in accordance with the Scriptures. (1 Cor 15:3–4)

I want you to notice the mention of the burial of Christ in this passage. What does it mean? I will tell you, and then I just want you to read the passage for yourselves to see whether you do not agree with me. When Paul mentions the burial, he means that the resurrection of Christ about which he is speaking is a bodily resurrection. The thing that was laid in the tomb in the burial was the body; and the thing that was laid in the tomb was the thing that came out of the tomb in the resurrection. "He died, he was buried, he rose." We follow here, as we read, what happened to the body of Jesus. If a man will just read the words without prejudice he will see that they are at this point as plain as day.

It is quite clear that Paul does not mean, and the Jerusalem church as quoted by him did not mean, that the body of Jesus remained in the tomb. The bodily resurrection is the only resurrection that the New Testament knows.

In fact, when we come to think about it, a resurrection that is not a bodily resurrection is a contradiction in terms. Did those first disciples, when they began the work of the Christian church, merely believe in the continued personal existence of Jesus? Was that what gave them their strange new confidence and power? Such a view is really quite absurd. They had *that* conviction even in the sad hours immediately after the crucifixion. They were not Sadducees. They believed in the personal survival of all men after death; and so they believed, even just after the crucifixion, in the personal survival of Jesus. But that conviction left them in despair. What changed their despair into joy was the substitution, in their minds, for a belief in the continued personal existence of Jesus, of a belief in his resurrection. It is quite absurd, then, to say that the two things, in their view, were the same. Our sources of information about the beginnings of the Christian church know nothing whatever of a resurrection that is not a bodily resurrection.

The second thing that I want you to notice in the report by Paul of the tradition of the Jerusalem church is the mention of the third day. "He was raised on the third day in accordance with the Scriptures," he says. There are few words in the whole Bible that are more uncomfortable to modern unbelief than those words "the third day" in the primitive Jerusalem tradition recorded here by Paul.

Those words demolish the whole edifice of the Galilean hypothesis as to the place of the appearances. They show, by the testimony of the very first disciples, that the first appearance did *not* take place in Galilee weeks after the crucifixion but on the third day and at Jerusalem. I know that attempts are made to evade the plain implications of these words. The first appearances, it is said, took place only weeks afterwards, but when they did take place the disciples who experienced them hit upon the notion that Jesus had risen long before and merely had not chosen to appear to them until then. But why in the world did they hit upon just the third day as the day of the resurrection if nothing in particular happened to them on that day? Various answers have been given to that question, but they are vain. No, the mention of a third day in the primitive Jerusalem tradition interposes a mighty barrier against the whole attempt to explain the appearances of the risen Christ as hallucinations experienced at a time when it would be too late to investigate the tomb of Jesus to see whether the resurrection had really happened or not.

The truth is that the origin of the church in Jerusalem is explicable if Jesus really rose from the dead, and it is not explicable if he did not so rise. The very existence of the Christian church is a mighty testimony to the resurrection of our Lord.

But, it will be objected, that is all very well, but the trouble is that the thing we are asked to believe is really unbelievable. We are asked to believe that a dead man rose from the dead, and we have never seen a man who did that.

What is our answer to this objection? It is very simple. You say, my friend, that you have never seen a man who rose from the dead after he had been laid really dead in the tomb? Quite right. Neither have I. You and I have never seen a man who rose from the dead. That is true. But what of it? You and I have never seen a man who rose from the dead; but then you and I have never seen a man like Jesus.

Do you not see, my friends? What we are trying to establish is not the resurrection of any ordinary man, not the resurrection of a man who is to us a mere x or y, not the resurrection of a man about whom we know nothing, but the resurrection of Jesus.

There is a tremendous presumption against the resurrection of any ordinary man, but when you come really to know Jesus as he is pictured to us in the Gospels you will say that whereas it is unlikely that any ordinary man should rise from the dead, in his case the presumption is exactly reversed. It is unlikely that any ordinary man should rise; but it is unlikely that *this* man should not rise; it may be said of this man that it was impossible that he should be holden of death.

The point is that this thing hangs together. We have in the Gospels an account of a person who was entirely unique. He was totally different from other men in his moral purity and strength. Yet he made the most stupendous claims—claims that place him beyond the bounds of sanity unless the claims were true. The claims are true if the resurrection really happened; they are a hopeless puzzle if the resurrection did not happen.

Do you see what I am driving at, my friends? The evidence of the truth of Christianity must be taken as a whole. The direct evidence for the resurrection must be taken together with the total picture of Jesus in the Gospels, and then that must be taken in connection with the evidence for the existence of God and the tremendous need of man which is caused by sin. If you take the Bible as a whole you have a grand consistent account of God, of the world, and of human life. If you reject the Bible, and particularly if you reject the fact of the resurrection, you have a jumble of meaningless and detached bits of information that dance before your imagination in a wild and riotous rout.

Oh, that God would open men's eyes that they might see, that they might detect the grand sweep and power of his testimony to himself in his Word! Oh, that he would take away the terrible blindness of men's minds! Has he taken away the blindness of *your* minds, my friends? Do you know the risen Christ today as your Savior and your Lord? If you do not yet know him, will you not bow before him at this hour and say, "My Lord and my God!"